Praise for W

I love *Wealth On Any* ▮ can become wealthy. I bc because it makes the journey to financial freedom one of seeming effortlessness.
- Mark Victor Hansen, co-creator, #1 *New York Times* Best-selling *Chicken Soup for the Soul®* series.

This is perhaps the most important subject you will ever deal with and *Wealth On Any Income* gives you a step-by-step roadmap to follow. You can achieve all your dreams of financial freedom by putting these ideas to work.
- Brian Tracy, America's #1 Training Authority. Author of *Maximum Achievement*, seven other books and 300 different audio and video learning programs.

You bring a unique point of view around money that has helped my business and me personally. Through your coaching, I have not only improved the management of my cash flow but also my relationship with money in general. I now have less stress, greater stability, more freedom and an enhanced sense of abundance. Thank you.
—Carl Zaiss, Trainer, Speaker, international business consultant to corporations such as T&T, General Motors and Sprint; co-author of *Sales Effectiveness Training*

The concepts and approach of *Wealth on Any Income* are ideal for those who have difficulty facing financial concerns through traditional approaches. I recommend this book to my clients.
—James W. Gottfurcht, Ph.D., author of *Financial Fitness: The Complete Workout Book*. Psychologist and consultant to the financial services industry and MasterCard International.

I have recommended *Wealth On Any Income* to my clients.
—Katherine M. Reider, Ph.D. Valley Counseling Center, Encino, CA

Your teaching style is clear and inspires confidence.
—Susan Patton, ACSW, LISW, CEAP President and Director, Employee Assistance Program, Inc., Hilton Head, South Carolina

I thank you for coming into my life. If I hadn't listened to every word of your tape program, I probably wouldn't be willing to face this mess head on. Your program will benefit any human being who does not know where his/her money comes from or where it goes.
—Constance Weatherman Bodywork- Practitioner, Marina del Rey, CA

Wealth On Any Income has the 'rubber meets the road' kind of tools that supported me to turn my balance sheet around completely from negative to positive in twelve months.
—Larry Salk, President, Ventana Systems Santa Monica, CA

I'm so excited, I don't know where to begin! Your 'money chat' with us that afternoon changed my life permanently! We are committed to getting totally out of debt by the end of 1997. I've already paid off all my department store credit cards.
—Erin Peary, President, LA DI DA, Ltd., Half Moon Bay, CA

We had a successful law practice, and we had approximately $160,000 of unsecured short-term debt. I quickly realized that my perception of our spending habits was dramatically different from reality. With your help, within two years our credit card debt had been completely eliminated. At the present time, our only short-term debt is a car loan.
—David Bilford, Esq., Van Nuys, CA

Wow, what a difference the right advice can make! Thanks to your coaching, this has turned into a breakthrough year. While I am grateful for the explosion in my production, I am more grateful for the long-term direction you have guided me to build into my business plan.

—Neal Kaye, Jr., Vice President, Private Client Group Merrill Lynch, New Orleans, Louisiana

Until I met with you, I spent at least two nights a week staying up late trying to figure out the best way to pay off my debt faster. After our meeting, I have been able to approach it from a completely new perspective. A goal that used to seem daunting is now possible and within sight. In addition, I received excellent advice on starting a professional project I have been considering for a long time.

—Rhonda Madden, ICM, Inc., Beverly Hills, CA

If you don't know where you want to go, you'll end up somewhere else. Don't take the financial journey through life without this roadmap. In just 12 easy to follow steps, Rennie Gabriel takes the mystery out of the road to financial freedom.

—Ginita Wall, CPA, CFP. Author of *Your Next Fifty Years: A Completely New Way to Look at How, When, and if You Should Retire.*

WEALTH
ON ANY
INCOME

12 Secrets to Your
Financial Freedom

RENNIE GABRIEL

GABRIEL
PUBLISHING

Wealth On Any Income, Revised: 12 Secrets to Your Financial Freedom

Cover and book design: Rebecca Hayes

Published in the United States by
Gabriel Publications
Encino, CA 91436
Ph: 818-990-8086
Email: Rennie@RennieGabriel.com
Website: www.RennieGabriel.com

ISBN: 978-1-891689-81-9

Library of Congress Catalog Number: 2014910588

Printed in the United States

Dedication

Dedicated to my wife Dianne and my children Ryan, Davida, my step-daughter Arielle, and my grandchildren. The best people anyone could have in their life. I love you all.

Table of Contents

About the Author

Rennie Gabriel is a UCLA instructor and award-winning author. His first edition of *Wealth On Any Income* was # 1 at Amazon in April of 2002. Rennie continues to provide public workshops and corporate training to empower people in the areas of time, money and productivity in their business and personal life. His range extends from working with organizations like the FBI, city governments and Fortune 500 corporations, to supporting individuals.

He is the President of The Financial Coach, Inc. and the retired owner of Gabriel Publications with over 80 titles on consumer education in bookstores. He is often on TV and radio, and quoted in media publications. He went from near bankruptcy in 1982 to financial independence in 1987, and repeated the process after two divorces. The goal for clients and students is to create work as a choice, not a requirement.

Rennie started in the financial services industry in 1972. He earned the Charter Life Underwriter (CLU) and Certified Financial Planner® (CFP) designations. He lives in Encino, CA, with his wife, Dianne. Rennie's two children are grown and he has four grandchildren. His son, Ryan, is a Chartered Financial Analyst (CFA) with the Private Banking Division of Wells Fargo and his daughter Davida is an attorney living in Las Vegas working as the Development Director of the Adelson Campus. His daughter-in-law, Rachel, is a psychologist and his son-in-law, Damon, has a livery business.

Rennie helped establish the International Association for Financial Planning chapter in the San Fernando Valley suburb of Los Angeles, of which he is Past-President.

He was Director of Pensions for USLife of California, and in 1983 with two other people, established his own pension firm, designing and administering qualified retirement plans for corporations all over Southern California. His firm was acquired by a public corporation in 1987.

i

For three years in the 1990's, Rennie was the Treasurer of the San Fernando Valley Employee Assistance Professionals Association (EAPA) and on their national finance committee. He is a past board member of the Apartment Association, listed in Who's Who in Finance and Industry, Who's Who in the West, and selected Man of the Year by The American Biographical Institute. He used to lecture for continuing education of attorneys and CPAs, and is a sought after speaker.

In 1993, Rennie introduced a program to more than 40 high school districts to teach students how to handle money effectively. He also provided the in-service training to high school teachers in accounting, finance and math for that program. Materials are still provided FREE to public or private high schools through an educational endowment.

With $16,000 in 2002, Rennie and his wife started buying small multi-unit residential properties. Based on property upgrades, tax deferred exchanges and effective property management, in 10 years the net worth of this real estate had grown to $3.2 million.

Introduction – Read this first!

Hello. I'm delighted you chose to open this book and see what's inside. And, if you continue to read and take actions on the exercises and tools provided, you can achieve financial independence. This is when work becomes a choice, and not a requirement. I still work because I love what I do, not because I have to earn money. I created this after struggling for years thinking that making more money would lead to financial independence. I was wrong, and you can use my experience, and the experience of the thousands of others with whom I have worked with, to avoid wasting your time and get on the fast track to wealth.

The first third of this book is about your feelings, attitudes, and values about money. If we don't address that first, then all of the great tips, advice, exercises, and tools in the other two-thirds of the book are just a waste of words, because you probably would not take action on any of it. Your beliefs can block you from taking the actions your intellect tells you are the right things to do.

It doesn't matter where you are now. You may be earning an excellent income but feel it's not enough. You may be struggling to get by and don't even know where to start. In 1998 I was practically broke. I had gotten divorced for the second time and had nothing more than a little equity in a rental property and about $2000 of cash to my name. My house was mortgaged to the max and with the credit card debt I had, if I sold the house I would walk away with about $500. That is not a typo; I did say five hundred dollars.

I first began writing this in the spring of 2008 and then set it aside for six years. It was at the time of a sub-prime mortgage crisis; the failure of Countrywide Mortgage, one of the country's largest home lenders; the failure of one of Wall Street's biggest brokerage houses, Bear Stearns; and the willingness of the Federal Reserve to make loans beyond the banks to securities firms. Foreclosures in California hit a record with 47,171 in the first three months of 2008. This is more than four times the number of foreclosures that occurred one year earlier. Default notices in the same period, which is the first step on the road to foreclosure, were at 110,000. This is an increase of 143% from the same period one year earlier and represents 1.4% of all the homes in California. About 68% of the default notices will end up as foreclosures. Even before the sub-prime mortgage meltdown is factored in, bankruptcies for 2007 increased by 38% to 850,912 for the year 2007 for individuals and businesses, with 96.6% representing individuals. In 2006 there were 617,660 bankruptcy filings.

By September 2008, Washington Mutual, the nation's largest savings and loan, and 6th largest bank, failed. Lehman Brothers brokerage failed. Merrill Lynch, the largest brokerage was taken over by Bank of America. The government said it would pump $700 BILLION to maintain confidence in the financial markets. In October Wells Fargo and Citibank were fighting over who would get Wachovia Bank. BIB

Let's face it; we went through tough economic times. It was not the first time, and it will not be the last time. When you have your finances in order, based on the principals in this book that have worked for 5000 years, you will be able to survive any economic meltdown. Most of the material from my award-winning book, *Wealth On Any Income*, which was a #1 selling book at www.Amazon.com in April of 2002, has been updated. Many thousands of copies have been sold over the years and I received many testimonials from insurance agents, stock brokers and entrepreneurs, and notable authors.

Here are two examples:

"I love this book. Everyone, that includes you, can become wealthy. I bought 100 copies of this book to give away because it makes the journey to financial freedom one of seeming effortlessness."
Mark Victor Hansen, co-creator, # 1 *New York Times* Bestselling *Chicken Soup for the Soul* ® series

"This is perhaps the most important subject you will ever deal with and this book gives you a step-by-step roadmap to follow. You can achieve all your dreams of financial freedom by putting these ideas to work."
- Brian Tracy, America's #1 Training Authority. Author of *Maximum Achievement*, seven other books and 300 different audio and video learning programs

Putting into practice the same concepts and material I use will allow you to prosper through any rollercoaster economic environment. You will be able to prosper in good and bad economic times. The point is; when you know how to handle money effectively, it does not matter what is going on in the economy. You will be able to save money, you will be able to invest money, and you will not have credit card debt.

In this book, I'll show you how to Move from Debt to Wealth, On Any Income. This is the name of the UCLA class I have been teaching since 1994. Following the same advice I give my students, I rebuilt my financial life to a greater wealth than I had prior to either of my divorces.

More importantly, testimonials have come from those for whom this book was written; ordinary working people who struggle from paycheck to paycheck, often struggling with credit card debt who feel like things have little hope of changing. Because of my presentations to corporations and other organizations, testimonials have come from the employees at the Los Angeles Department of Water and Power, the FBI, Toyota Motors, Ford, the US Postal Service, Fox Television, HBO, Cal-Tech, UCLA, Union Bank, Transamerica Insurance, and other groups plus the tenants of the apartment buildings owned or controlled by the various entities we have set up.

This book can be of assistance to everyone, from the person who received no instructions from either their school or their parents to professional financial planners and accountants. How can that be? Easy. It's written in a simple, practical, and step-by-step approach. Anyone who can read at a sixth grade level and knows how to add, subtract, multiply and divide will be able to work with this material.

Whether people have a Ph.D. in economics, or didn't finish high school, they can create value from this book. This book is about the basics. The greatest athletes in any sport have the best grasp of the basics. Basics are the strong foundation upon which they built their success. If you have already mastered the basics of handling money effectively and you have created financial prosperity for yourself, then you can use this book to teach others how to do it because it provides the 12 steps to creating wealth using a systematic approach. Those of you who have created financial prosperity will quickly recognize the value in this book and can create additional value for yourself. This book is for people who want to have both spiritual and financial wealth.

This book is for people who want to **have** financial wealth. While this book can be used by people who want *others to think they have wealth*, that is not my purpose. I'm referring to the people who want to impress others. We all want to do that to some extent, but I'm referring to those who are living beyond their means so that others will think they are successful. My intention is to support those who want the security and peace of mind that comes from having money in the bank, stocks, bonds, mutual funds or income-producing real estate. You may be living paycheck-to-paycheck now and perhaps you want to have a business which generates an income whether you're present at the business or not, knowing if you chose not to work, you don't have to. You may want to buy a new car and pay cash for it. You might want to have the money to travel anywhere in the world and choose if you will go or not. Maybe you want to buy a home for yourself or your children. All of this is possible and possible for YOU.

What do I mean by wealth on any income? It doesn't mean your debts will be gone instantly, like the mortgage on a house, your car loan, or other debts. It means you will see how you can live within your income, payoff your debts and begin the path to creating financial independence or financial freedom in any economic environment. Again, I define this as the ability to choose to work or not work. This happens when your financial needs are met by your money working for you, instead of you working for money. This is where work **becomes a choice and not a requirement**.

In this program you'll learn a process of combining three things: Awareness, Tools and Actions to create financial prosperity. It incorporates using The Financial Coach Spending Plan Checkbook Register to track expenses and measure the level of pleasure you get when you spend your money. This system requires you to treat yourself like you deserve to own some of the money you earn, and I'll ask you to take actions consistent with your values in order to achieve financial independence.

There are two ways this book can serve you. First, you can just read it to get some new and valuable information. Or, you can use the tools I provide and make powerful new decisions. It doesn't take a rocket scientist to figure out you'll get far more from using the tools and applying the skills than just reading the book.

Don't let the word tools concern you. I use this word to describe the forms and concepts I've provided. If you wanted to prepare a gourmet meal you would need cooking tools, also called utensils, like a knife, spatula, grater, pot, pan and so on. If you wanted to repair a car you would need things like a wrench, screwdriver and pliers. (When I was young, car repair tools were chewing gum and wire.) If you wanted to build a house you would need a hammer, nails and a saw. As you use the tools in this book, you will be developing the skills to build a financial house; one that will shelter you from fear, anxiety or concerns about your economic circumstances regardless of what is happening in the general economy.

Also, as you read, think about others. You may hold the key to the financial growth of someone else. My agenda is for everyone to have financial prosperity easily and effortlessly. And, when you've created it for yourself, I feel you have an obligation to help others. Not only that, but helping someone else achieve their goals makes it easier for you to achieve yours. You will see how this works in the section on coaching.

You may think you're the only one with financial concerns. Or, even if you know others are having difficulty, it's not likely you talk about it in any detail. This program has assisted thousands of people to overcome difficult financial issues. It has helped people from a wide range of occupations. You may not have realized this, but just because someone like a doctor, financial planner or CPA knows how to do things for other people, like heal them or take care of their investments or taxes, doesn't mean they've done what they need to do for themselves.

You may be wondering where I get off writing about wealth on any income. Besides my financial mess in 1998 after my second divorce, I was also flat broke 16 years earlier. I was struggling in my own business and I had to take soda pop bottles to the grocery store for food. I was three months behind on my mortgage payments and the bank was preparing to take away my house. My wife and children were at their wit's end. I was selling poster art at the time, more like a salesman than a business owner, and obviously not a good one. I was at least smart enough to figure out this wasn't working.

I returned to selling pension and profit-sharing plans, and with the help of two other people formed a pension administration company. After four years, we negotiated the purchase of our company to a division of a public corporation. I became financially independent at age 39, and it didn't take millions of dollars to do it. In addition to the equity in my home and one rental property, I was able to choose work, or no work, with $300,000 of additional cash. I invested this money and produced $60,000 per year of income and, based on my lifestyle at the time, I could cover my expenses whether I worked or not. Creating the money you want can be done either all at once, or little by little, which is how most people do it. If your lifestyle would require $3 million or $30 million, you'll see how to do that, too.

Then in 1987 I got divorced, and this cut into the investment that created my income. I remarried a couple of years later and then got divorced again in 1997. By now my net worth had been cut in half, and then cut in half again. As I said earlier, in 1998 I was practically broke. But the principals that you will read about in this book do work, and I am married for the last time. And using the principals in the book I built up my wealth to a multi-million dollar level in just six years. I am not special; I am average. You can choose to apply these principals and prosper, or you can choose to continue doing what you have been doing, and continue to get what you have gotten.

An Overview of the Twelve Steps

Now, let's get to the twelve steps to financial independence. Sometimes I call these secrets, but they shouldn't be. They are based on concepts from many books, and some of them I will mention as we go along. The following books are highly recommended: *Couples and Money* by Victoria Collins; *Rich Dad, Poor Dad* by Robert Kiyosaki; *Your Money or Your Life* by Dominguez and Robin; *The Richest Man in Babylon* by George Clason; *Wishcraft, How to Get What You Really Want* by Barbara Sher; *How to Get Out of Debt* by Jerrold Mundis and *The Millionaire Next Door* by Stanley and Danko.

This book is laid out in three sections. The first two sections, or almost half the book, are about your feelings, attitudes, beliefs, and values about money. Again, if we don't first deal with how you feel about money, then all of the great tools, tips and techniques would just be a waste of words because you probably wouldn't take any actions or put any of those tools into use.

7

In Section 1, you will have the opportunity to examine what makes you tick. You will see the attitudes and beliefs that may have held you back. You establish goals based on your values. You will be able to achieve them because they are based on who you are. This is the most important part of the book. This is what the UCLA students and the participants in my workshops say make it all worthwhile. This is the part where you get the motivation and inspiration to use the tools you will learn.

You may have a financial problem, and then you learn *how* to solve it. Big deal! What *reason* do you have to do it? The reason is created in the first part of the book. This is where you will be inspired to write your goals; the things you want to have and how you want your life to be. You will create *your* reasons for using the tools you'll be provided. If you want to have work as a choice and not a requirement, you're reading the right book. Even if you just want to end the day-to-day struggle over money, or get out of credit card debt, you're reading the right book

In the first section of the book you'll set up a method for writing long-term goals and create the action *structure* to achieve them. I want to emphasize **structure**. Results are not produced just by taking random actions, but by taking actions *within a framework designed to produce a specific result*. This is what I refer to as an ***Action Structure to Produce Results***. You'll learn how to write a goal *from* the future, not *for* the future.

I will talk about some things you've probably not read about anywhere else that will provide the motivation for you to go after your goals and use the tools provided. You'll learn about the two ingredients most often missing in goal setting workshops and books. I'll give you these two powerful items that are responsible for 90% of the success that people achieve.

My objective is for everyone who reads this book to eliminate unsecured debt (credit cards), if they have any, and create financial freedom; the choice to work or not work. Or, pursue your passion regardless of the income it will generate. Many of the tenants to whom I have given copies of this book have ended up moving out of our apartments and purchased their own home.

That thrills me. If any of this is what you want, hang on, and get ready to have it happen.

The Inspiration and Action Structure

In Section II we look at how we find the inspiration to take the actions to produce results and achieve our goals, and we also need to know the roadblocks to financial success and understanding the difference between good debt and bad debt. I'm going to be talking about the challenges we face financially. As an example, bad debt will have you suffer and good debt will set you free. These challenges are based on an inability to handle money effectively, whether due to our emotional reactions or lack of education. We're going to use the word *challenges* for what most people see as *problems*. I want to emphasize the importance of the words we use, and get off on the right foot to start with.

The words we use have a direct impact on how we feel about things, situations, people and so on. If I talk about having hope rather than confidence I create two different images. When I say you face a financial problem rather than a financial challenge, you will probably have less desire to face the problem, but more willingness to overcome the challenge.

In this section, you'll see the challenges you need to overcome.

Some parts of the book are not pleasant to read. But unless you know the problems or challenges, how could you possibly prepare for them, and solve them? We'll discuss the results of a lack of education or a lack of discipline, and it's not pleasant. So, just bear with me, it gets much, much, better.

To make you feel better, let me ask you a few questions: First, can you recall when you were in high school? Did you have a class that taught you how to handle money effectively? Probably not. I've asked this question to thousands of people and only 3 or 4 people out of every hundred people say they learned how to handle money from some high school class. Next

9

question: Can you recall when you were of high school age having your parents instruct you on how to handle money effectively? Again, probably not. I get a similar small percentage, about 4-6%, who say their parents taught them anything about handling money.

Unfortunately, when people tell me what they got from their parents, most often I hear things like: "My mom told me to spend less than I earn," or "My dad said, 'If you don't have the money, don't buy it, and don't use credit,' or "My parents said, 'Save something from everything you earn.'" You need to understand, these aren't instructions. These are what I call admonitions. They might as well have said, "Be good!" It's like throwing you in the water and then saying, "Swim!" With those kinds of statements our parents made, they contained no instructions on *how* to be good, or swim, or *how* to live on less than we earn. Please, don't think I'm blaming parents. What were they supposed to do? They did the best they could and they couldn't give you information they didn't have.

The Tools

In Section III, we will deal with steps five through twelve. You will be provided the information you should have been given in high school, or by your parents, but didn't get. Included in this section are *the tools*. This is the information we ought to have been provided. This is the information to which I say everyone is entitled. It's not your fault if you're having problems handling money effectively and getting what you want. You haven't been given the tools to do any better.

We will go over the tools you can use to overcome the challenge. These are the same tools the wealthiest people in this country use. As documented in the book *The Millionaire Next Door* by Stanley and Danko, these are the tools millionaires used to become wealthy and the tools they use to stay that way. When William Danko interviewed me for his next book, I saw how I was beginning to take for granted how easy it became to create wealth when using those tools. But those tools, the same ones that are in this book, allowed me to stay on track.

You'll learn how to payoff consumer debt and set up a spending plan. This is a plan to *spend* money, not budget, and reach your financial goals. You'll learn how to project expenses and income, find out where your money goes, and have the tools which will make it possible to live within your income in 90 days, *guaranteed!* And, you do not have to be a math wiz to understand how this works.

Whether you are a business owner or individual, you do not need any financial background to do anything in this book. If you do have a financial background, you'll instantly recognize the value of the simple approach I've taken. You'll learn how to choose powerfully from the products, companies, and advertising that scream for your attention. You'll learn how to measure the level of pleasure you're getting for the money you're spending. In this way, you'll be able to align your values with how you spend your money and reach your goals.

You will discover the way to create financial independence through a method called 'Pay Yourself First.' You may have heard about this before, but not the way I'll talk about it. This concept has worked for over 5,000 years and it still works today. Dr. Jerry Buss said this is what he did. He worked 6 days and lived on 5 days income. He saved that extra day of income and used his savings to invest and then bought the Los Angeles Forum, the Lakers basketball team, and the Kings hockey team. The last part of the book will illustrate the magic of compound earnings. You'll read about what this means to you in creating financial independence and achieving your goals from part one.

Let's use an analogy: Say you have some lumber, which we'll call a raw material. Plus, you have some tools, such as a hammer, saw and nails. And, you have someone available with expert advice. What are some of the things you could build? You could build a house, boat, fence, apartment building, furniture, bridge or whatever. Practically anything. Right? (Howard Hughes built the Spruce Goose. It may be the largest airplane ever built, and it was made from wood.)

What if you still had the lumber and expert advice, but chose not to use the tools? What could you build? Practically nothing. Right? Well, you have the raw intelligence to create financial freedom. I'm going to supply the tools and expert advice. You can choose to use the tools or not. The financial house you build will be based on whether or not you choose to use the tools provided.

These next few paragraphs may alter your life, regardless of what you do with this book. It involves how to read, or how to listen, to any material or information that may be familiar to you. There are two ways to pay attention to familiar information: You can either make statements, or you can ask questions.

An example of something familiar could be that you are aware you will not have the money to cover your bills in full this month. You could make a statement like, "I'll have more money next month." The statement may be wishful thinking. Regardless, it will not produce any thoughts or actions to create a change in your situation.

Instead, I'm requesting you ask yourself a question such as, "What do I need to do to have more money next month?" The question could create answers that could move you to action and create the changes to your situation. Statements rarely produce anything other than agreement or disagreement. Questions produce answers. And answers to your financial concerns could lead you to the financial freedom you're seeking.

I request that you ask yourself questions as you read this book, such as, "How can I use this in my situation? Where can I go to get what I need? Who can I work with to support me in getting what I want? What can I do to create the changes I want to have in my life?" Taking action on the answers to questions like these can alter your life forever. -Rennie Gabriel, May 2014

Section I -

Beliefs, Values and Attitudes

HAPPINESS

If you deliberately plan to be less than you are capable of being, then I warn you that you'll be unhappy for the rest of your life. You will be evading your own capacities, your own possibilities.
—Abraham Maslow

Step 1.

Identify Your Beliefs and Values

Belief Statements We Need To Deal With

To create wealth, the first place to start is with our attitudes, beliefs and values. There are some beliefs that hold us back. These beliefs keep us stuck in the same old rut of living from paycheck to paycheck, choosing which bills we can pay this month, and being concerned about impressing strangers. It's been said 85% of working Americans are three paychecks away from insolvency. (This is when someone doesn't have enough money to pay their bills.) It's our limiting beliefs that have us stuck in jobs we hate in order to pay for the things Madison Avenue has convinced us we need. We are going to go over some of these beliefs, but first we need to lay the foundation of what impacts the actions we take.

There are three areas from which we can operate when we're making decisions: our thoughts, our feelings and/or our values. I'll use health as an example to demonstrate operating from these three different areas. A thought could sound like, "I think I'll start exercising tomorrow morning by jogging." The next morning feelings could sound like, "It's dark, I'm cold and I don't feel like exercising. I feel like sleeping longer." A value could be a statement like, "My body is a temple" or "My health is a top priority above all else" or "No amount of money can buy health."

In the above example, would I go jogging if I operated from the feeling level? Of course not. Feelings are far more powerful than thoughts, and most people operate from their feelings most of the time. Thoughts are like New Year's resolutions, they disappear quickly. Feelings are one of our most powerful motivators.

Primarily, we operate from our desire to gain pleasure or our desire to avoid pain. If you have read this far you are looking to create a change in your life. Either you were in pain about your financial situation, or you thought you could create a more abundant life if you had more information. If all you operate from is your thoughts or feelings however, you will not be able to achieve the level of success from this book which you desire. And, isn't achieving success probably the reason you continued reading?

The most powerful dimension from which to operate is the area of values. This is the area where you look inside and say who you are. Are you a person of integrity? Do you make promises and keep them? Is freedom the most important thing to you? Or, is it family, spirituality, community, money, prestige, love, wisdom or security? Who you say you are and what's important to you are a reflection of your values. Values make up your internal beliefs. They establish what you say is "right" and "wrong," "good" and "bad," what you should or should not do, who you say you are as a person, and who you say you are not. When you violate your values, you experience pain in your life. Most people will punish themselves in some manner such as worry, guilt, or set up a situation where they are exposed and punished by someone else. When your behavior matches your values, you experience happiness or contentment.

This is the area for you to tap into to create the level of financial abundance and freedom you want plus use the steps and tools in this book. At the end of this step, you'll have a chance to identify your values.

If health is one of my fundamental values, then just because I wake up one morning and don't feel like exercising, the feeling won't stop me. One of the funniest experiences that demonstrated this for me occurred while I was exercising one morning. I was jogging about two blocks from my house when the following started going through my head, "I don't feel like jogging this morning. I'm not in the mood. I want to go back to bed." I couldn't help but laugh at what was going on in my head. Here I was in the act of taking care of my body through exercise while my mind is telling me it doesn't feel like doing this. It was too late, I was already exercising, and I went on to complete 5 kilometers. When you operate from your values, you can think or feel whatever you want, but you don't have to act on those silly thoughts or useless feelings. Those feelings would not assist me in maintaining my health.

Beliefs are like the thoughts or feelings we've heard from others and may have adopted for ourselves. Here are some of the thoughts/beliefs which can keep us from creating financial prosperity and freedom.

Thought/Belief #1
More money will buy the happiness I'm missing now.

Just saying this reminds most people of the adage "Money can't buy happiness." And, it doesn't matter if you think you know where to shop for it. What money buys is "pleasure," not "happiness." Most people confuse these two feelings. "Happiness" can come from what we do for others. What we do for others creates a state of contentment and well-being about who we are. I'm not talking about dysfunctional co-dependency; I'm talking about our contributions to other human beings.

"Pleasure" comes from what we receive. A day at Disneyland can give us pleasure; gifts give us pleasure, a massage, a round of golf, a shopping trip to the mall. These give us pleasure. They are short term and fleeting. Most people mistakenly think the next outfit they buy will make them happy, even though the 14 outfits they bought before didn't. What they bought was fleeting pleasure.

Have you ever been in a conversation with someone who was upset about something, or just maybe down in the dumps? And, as a result of talking with you, sharing their feelings, understanding what they were going through, they felt better. Think about something similar where you helped someone out by being there for them, but it didn't involve spending any money. Could you say that experience made you feel happy? You see, it doesn't cost any money to create happiness. It's internally generated based on what we're dong for other people. Pleasure comes from what others are doing for us, or what we're doing or buying for ourselves. It's external and fleeting. How important is the value of happiness to you?

However, we all need a certain level of income to maintain the lifestyle we believe is appropriate: To have comfortable shelter; wholesome and nourishing food; clothe our children decently, and so on. The difficulty is defining what is appropriate. We deserve as much pleasure as possible from the money we spend. The only way to know if we are getting the pleasure we seek is to measure it. While this is only subjective, you get to be the one doing the evaluation. And, the only way we can measure it is to track it. This is one of the requests I will make in the next section under "Tools."

In the book Your Money or Your Life, Joe Dominguez and Vicki Robin talk about this idea. They also bring up the conversation about what money represents. They say it represents the life energy you give up in exchange for money. You can then evaluate the pleasure you get by how much of your life you gave up. Is another powder blue sweater worth 25 hours of your working life? Would you buy this if you didn't have to work for a living? These are the types of questions you can use to measure the level of pleasure you're getting for what you're paying.

Thought/Belief #2
Budgets and spending plans are the same thing.

No, they're not. In this program I talk about spending plans, and I say it's different from a budget. A spending plan is based on how much money you want to spend in some area or category of your life. It is not based on how much money you will be restricted to, as in a budget. For many people the word "budget" is like the word "diet." What are the first three letters of the word diet? "D I E." That's got to be real exciting. Yeah, you're looking forward to budgeting, just like you'd look forward to a diet or a funeral.

What we're doing here is finding out where our money is going so we can determine if we're getting the level of satisfaction we're paying for. A spending plan is based on our values. It's based on the long term goals and objectives we've created, again, based on our values. It's designed to monitor and support us in spending money in alignment with our goals, objectives and values.

Thought/Belief #3
If I just made more money, I wouldn't need a spending plan or budget.

This attitude is based on the idea that more money solves the problems of mismanagement. It doesn't. How much money you earn is not as important as what you do with it. Look in the newspaper and read the articles of lottery winners who go bankrupt. They didn't have the skills to manage before they won millions. How did winning millions of dollars give them the skills? It didn't. Within three years over 70% of those who won the California Lottery were in debt beyond their winnings.

I have an issue of People magazine dated February 24, 1997. On the cover it shows six entertainment stars who have gone broke, and one of them earned $33 million per year! People can outspend any amount of money they receive. Having more money is not the solution—handling expenses in alignment with your values and goals is the solution. Then you can create more money and have it produce the results you want.

Thought/Belief #4
This will take too much time and restrict my spending.

Are you willing to spend 5–10 seconds to see where your money goes? One of the key concepts of this program is Tool #5; the Spending Plan Register. It only takes 5–10 seconds to complete, after any expenditure, and provides you with all of the data you could want. In talking with thousands of people, I have run across very few who were not willing to spend 5–10 seconds to know where their money goes. It does not restrict your spending. It only creates awareness. You still choose how and where you will spend your money. Only now the decisions become conscious, not unconscious or pre-programmed. Do you value knowledge or ignorance?

Thought/Belief #5
Setting up a spending plan will be too complicated.

Is this your concern? Can you read and write? Can you add and subtract? If so, you have all the skills necessary to set up and operate my Financial Coach Spending Plan system. It won't be complicated because I'll lead you by the hand and show you what's necessary.

Thought/Belief #6
Rich people don't have to do this. I shouldn't have to either.

The difficulty with this belief is it's a two-part comment, and both assumptions are false. Most of the assumptions we have about millionaires are incorrect according to the book, The Millionaire Next Door by Stanley and Danko. They have studied millionaires for over 20 years, and this book documents their findings. To quote from the book on page 40:

They became millionaires by budgeting and controlling expenses, and they maintain their affluent status the same way.

To make this more clear, they provide the following analogy: Have you ever noticed those people whom you see jogging day after day? They are the ones who seem not to need to jog. But that's why they are fit. Those who are wealthy work at staying financially fit. But those who are not financially fit do little to change their status.

Poverty and Prosperity Thinking

Another layer of attitudes and beliefs could be described as poverty or prosperity thinking. Some of the previous beliefs we've covered could be based on an attitude where an individual feels like it doesn't matter what they do; that it won't make a difference. This can be illustrated in both negative and positive terms. In poverty thinking, people could say to themselves, "It doesn't matter how much money I earn, I'll never have anything left over." If someone is operating from a prosperity consciousness they could be saying things like, "It doesn't matter what I do, I know it will turn out profitably," or "Things always seem to go my way, I always have enough."

James W. Gottfurcht, Ph.D. (pronounced "got-first"), a Brentwood (Los Angeles), California psychologist, has done extensive work in this area, and even has a business called Psychology of Money Consultants. He is a speaker and consultant to the financial service and credit industries, including MasterCard; teaches at UCLA, and has a private counseling practice.

Dr. Gottfurcht compares the damage poverty thinking can do to an individual's financial plans and activities as holes in a financial vessel. It doesn't matter how beautiful your ship is and it doesn't matter what material the hull is made of. It could be manufactured from the finest titanium metals in the most efficient aerodynamic design, but with holes in the hull it will not perform to its peak and could ultimately sink. The titanium hull and design represent prosperity thinking while the holes, which could let in the damaging water, represent poverty thinking.

What's to be done? Address the stinking thinking, face the demons and be aware of the sabotaging attitudes we may hold.

How is this done? Look over the following messages which may have been handed to you in the past, perhaps as a child, and determine if you buy into any of them. This is my interpretation of information gleaned from Financial Fitness: The Complete Workout Book by James W. Gottfurcht, Ph.D. (Reprinted with permission.)

"Rich people are unhappy." This communicates that it is better not to be rich and if you acquire wealth, you will regret it. It's like saying, "Money is bad."

"Money isn't important." This encourages people not to fully value themselves or their time and effort. Although money is not all important while self-esteem, health and free time are very important, money often plays a significant role in the creation of health, free time and self-esteem.

"Don't make mistakes." This says mistakes are bad. Not only are mistakes okay, they are necessary for learning and development. Mistakes are our best teachers, and in the world of money and investing, calculated risk-taking requires mistakes.

"You're not good in math." This communicates that you are not okay with numbers or counting, both of which are basic financial skills. There could be a hidden and/or unconscious agenda for a parent to say this to a child, or a mate to say this to their partner. It could also show up in statements like, "Don't worry your pretty little head about money," "I'll always take care of you." These comments communicate you don't have to be responsible for yourself. Mommy, daddy or a spouse will always be there to rescue you. It sets up a condition where a person can grow into adulthood and still be dependent on the parent(s) or spouse so they will continue to feel needed. While these "benefactors" complain about their "dependents" being unable to take care of themselves, they set up the condition, and wouldn't have it any other way.

For every poverty message, there can be a prosperity message as well. Some of the most powerful messages follow. If they were not said to you in the past, you can say them to yourself now. You can read them to yourself now or imagine an ideal person telling them to you now.

"I love you unconditionally." This says you are loved for who you are, regardless of how you think, feel or behave. There is no greater gift you can give to anyone, including yourself. If a child misbehaves, regardless of age, you can still disapprove of the behavior while still valuing, respecting and loving them as a person. An unconditionally loved child will learn to respect and trust themselves. They will be optimistic, attain what is within their reach and attract people and success.

"I believe in you." This message is strong, but not as powerful as "I love you." The individual will feel respected, trusted and cared for. They will feel encouraged to risk, experiment and develop into all they can become. You're telling them how you feel about their ability to get the task done.

"You can do it." This is a variation of "I believe in you" where the emphasis is placed on the person to whom you're speaking. You're telling the person they are able and have whatever they need to accomplish the goal.

Other prosperity messages show up in unexpected areas, like the children's book The Little Engine That Could where we hear, "I think I can. I think I can." Be aware of both the messages you speak as well as the ones you play in your head. Are you programming yourself for poverty or prosperity?

Let's examine what it looks like, or what it takes to be a millionaire. Much of it is based on the attitudes we have bought into. Following, is a quiz I developed from the book The Millionaire Next Door. Have fun and test what you think millionaires are like.

The Millionaire Quiz

Many people who purchase the *Wealth on Any Income* cassette tape or CD program, or take the "How to Be Rich on Any Income" workshop want to get out of economic difficulties and create financial security. Most people believe having a lot of money would provide the economic security they're looking for. The key is how to create it. Many people think they know what someone looks like who has the economic security they want, like a millionaire. This is someone who has a net worth of $1,000,000 or more. To see if you would recognize the typical millionaire, have fun with the quiz on the next page. (Typical means at least 50% share this trait.)

The typical millionaire is:

1. Age: ___ 57 ___ 45 ___ 72
2. Occupation:
___ Professional ___ Executive ___ Entrepreneur
3. Home Value:
___ $900,000 ___ $500,000 ___ $300,000
4. Automobile:
___ Rolls Royce ___ Mercedes, or other foreign
___ American made
5. Wealth came from:
___ Inheritance ___ Investments ___ Business/career
6. Work week:
___ 30–38 hours ___ 39–44 hours ___ 45–55 hours
7. Savings habits:
___ 20% of household income ___ 10–20% ___ 5–10%
8. Household income:
___ $500,000 – $900,000/year
___ $250,000 – $500,000/year
___ $100,000 – $250,000/year
9. Highest price paid for:
Suit: ___ $1,400 Shoes: ___ $650 Wristwatch: ___ $5,300
___ $ 600 ___ $200 ___ $1,000
___ $ 300 ___ $100 ___ $ 200

10. Primary credit card held:
___American Express Green ___American Express Gold
___Visa/ MasterCard ___Upscale department store
11. Investment trading:
___daily ___weekly ___monthly ___annually or less
Source: *The Millionaire Next Door*, Stanley & Danko, 1996
Answers: 1. Age 57 2. Entrepreneur 3. $300,000 4. American made 5. Business/career 6. 45–55 7. 20% 8. $100-250k 9. suit: $300, shoes: $100, watch: $200 10. Visa/MC 11. annual

WANTS
Men do not attract that which they want, but that which they are.
—*James Allen*

Money Beliefs Exercise for Couples

Now that you've had a chance to look at your beliefs about what millionaires are supposed to look like and how we may be carrying poverty or posterity thinking, let's find out where some of these beliefs may have come from. The following questions are from the book Couples and Money by Victoria F. Collins, reprinted with permission.

Bringing out your hidden money beliefs will help you understand where your attitudes, habits and money peculiarities come from. With these items out in the open, you have the ability to choose to keep them or discard them. You can choose new beliefs to replace old ones. The key here is choice. In knowing your beliefs, you can take responsibility for them and avoid blaming your partner, parent, or anyone else as though they have control over you.

Please answer the following questions by writing down your answers. If you are married or have a partner, it is important for each of you to write down your answers separately.

- What was my mother's role concerning finances?
- How is my role like hers?
- What was my father's role concerning finances?
- How is my role like his?

- As a child, did I think I was rich, poor, or middle class?
- How do those feelings affect me now?
- What were the main messages my parents gave me regarding money? How closely do I follow them, or rebel against them today?
- What are the main money traumas I've experienced?
- What lessons did I learn from them?
- How have those lessons altered the way I deal with money now?
- What big money successes have I had?
- What lessons did I learn from them?
- How have those lessons altered the way I deal with money now?
- What is my greatest fear regarding money?
- The last time I trusted someone with money I (they) . . .
- In thinking about all the things I do (or could do) with money, what makes me the most uncomfortable?
- What gives me the greatest pleasure?
- Are my partner and I well matched in money values?
- On what do we agree? Disagree?
- Now when I think of money, I see it as . . .
- When I chat with my peers, they say this about money...
- Are the beliefs and fears reflected in my answers serving me in my present circumstances?
- Which attitudes do I want to hold on to?
- Which ones do I want to change, or discard?
- How do these attitudes help or hurt my relationship?

Reprinted with permission from Victoria F. Collins.

Determine Your Values

Values: The ideals, customs, or institutions of a society toward which the people of the group, or an individual, hold in high regard. These values may be positive, such as cleanliness, freedom, education, or negative such as cruelty, crime or greed.

Value: An intrinsic excellence or desirability. The quality that renders it desirable or useful.

Principle(s): A personal or specific basis of conduct or management. A guiding sense of the requirements and obligations of right conduct. Used as a rule, implying a standard or test for guiding conduct or practices. A fundamental truth which may be used in deciding conduct or choice.

As we discussed earlier in the book, to create the level of power needed to change past attitudes and actions for the long term, you must operate from your values. Some consider these to be the principles they use to guide their actions. To determine your values, or principles, ask yourself any of the following questions and write down your answer on a separate sheet of paper. If you can't come up with an answer easily, you can look over the list of values that follow.

Values exercise questions:

- What's most important to me in my life?
- What's most important to me in (fill in any area you want: relationships, business, work, community)?
- What are five values I would use to describe who I am?

(Example: I would say I appreciate beauty, I am honest, thoughtful of others...)

After listing several values, ask yourself the following questions: "If I could only have one, which would it be?" "If I could only have one more, which would it be?" This will establish the priority of your values. Another way is to look at the list you made and continue to choose among two at a time to establish which is more important. Example: If I listed integrity, helping others, freedom, wisdom and stability as my values, I would use the following method to prioritize them: If I had to choose between freedom and helping others which would I choose? If I had to choose between freedom and wisdom, which would I choose? If I had to choose between helping others and wisdom, which would I choose? Go through each value and be sure you match it against each other value to determine which one you would have first, second, third and so on.

Please use a separate sheet of paper to write your values or principles from the previous values exercise questions. You can select from the following list of values if you need help.

Please do not look at this list until you have tried to do the values exercise first.

ACCOMPLISHMENT: Aspiring for excellent, making a lasting contribution.

ADVENTURE: Seeking thrills and excitement.

AESTHETICS: Appreciating beauty, art, music and so on.

AFFECTION: Love; being intimate and sensitive to another.

APPEARANCE: Physical attractiveness, sex appeal.

COMMUNITY: Participation in a social, business or geographic group.

COMPETITION: Winning, enjoying games against opponents.

COOPERATION: Participating with others, involved in team.

CREATIVITY: Being innovative, imaginative, solving problems.

DEVOTION: Strong, spiritual beliefs, faith, transcending self.

ECONOMIC SECURITY: Comfortable life, freedom from economic worry.

EDUCATION: Having a high level of training and culture; being well-informed.

EMOTIONAL WELL-BEING: Peace of mind, contentment.

EXCITEMENT: Adventure, new experiences, challenge.

EXPERTNESS: Being considered an authority.

FAMILY: Taking care of loved ones.

FREEDOM: Capacity to exercise free will; control one's path.

FRIENDSHIP: Closely knowing and being known by others.

HEALTH: Physical well-being.

HELPING OTHERS: Service and concern for the less fortunate, assuming social responsibility.

HONESTY: Being truthful and open with others.

INTEGRITY: Soundness of moral character.

INTELLECT: Using one's mind, acquiring knowledge.

LEADERSHIP: Being influential, persuasive, in command.

LOVE: Feelings of warm attachment and strong affection toward others; a desire for others' well-being.

LOYALTY: Sense of duty to others.

MONEY: Acquiring wealth.

PERSONAL GROWTH: Developing and using one's potential.

PLAY: Having fun; enjoying sports, games and so on.

POWER: Ability to dominate or control others; position of authority.

PRESTIGE: Gaining fame, respect, admiration.

PROMOTIONS: Career advancement.

RELIGION: Devotion to specific organized beliefs, practices or worship of god(s).

SECURITY: Free of danger, excitement or anxiety; firmly fixed.

SELF-ACCEPTANCE: Comfort with one's own strengths and limits.

SELF-CONFIDENCE: Faith in own talents and abilities.

SELF-CONTROL: Ability to inhibit expression of undesirable feelings and behaviors.

SEX: Seeking, enjoying physical pleasure.

SPIRITUALITY: Influenced by sacred or divine belief in the soul or god within all.

STABILITY: Order, predictability, an individual or world at peace.

STATUS: Position or rank of self in relationship to others.

WEALTH: Acquiring money and physical possessions.

WISDOM: Acquiring or possessing understanding and insight.

Section II

The Inspiration and Action Structure

SUCCESS

One may err in many ways, but be right in only one: which is why it is easy to fail, but difficult to succeed.
- Aristotle

(During his work to create the light bulb) I have not failed. I've just found 10,000 ways that won't work.

And

Our greatest weakness lies in giving up. The most certain way to succeed is always to try just one more time.
Thomas A. Edison

The Inspiration and Action Structure to Create Wealth

This is the section where the rubber hits the road; it separates the men from the boys, the women from the girls; a stitch in time saves nine; a bird in the hand is worth a bush... This is what I say (and most workshop participants agree) is the critical part of the program. In the introduction we discovered the challenge to creating financial freedom; a lack of education. We will address this again in Section II. Plus, I will provide the tools to overcome the challenge: A form to list and pay off credit card debt, create a Spending Plan, use a Spending Plan Checkbook Register, pay yourself first, allocate money for the expenses which show up on a sporadic basis, and use time and the tax laws to your investing advantage.

In this first section, we're going to talk about developing the motivation to use these tools. And before we get to that, I'm going to tell you a joke. It's about a guy sitting at a bar who says half to himself and half in prayer, "I'm really up the creek. I'm broke, no job, and the rent's due. If only I could come up with an idea, some kind of gimmick to make money."

Off to his right he hears a sound. It's coming from a shellfish, and it says, "Hey! Hey, Mac. Look at me! I'm the world's only talking clam!"

The guy at the bar responds, "Geesh, and I thought I had problems."

Sometimes we're so stuck in our own problems, we can't even see the solutions we've asked for.

I want to remind you again how to read what's coming up next. There are two ways. You can make statements like, "I know about this stuff," which closes your mind to creative solutions. Or, you can ask questions like, "How can I use this to accomplish what I want?" If you're willing to ask questions as you read familiar information, you'll be able to bring in the power of your mind to overcome the challenge of creating financial freedom. It's likely there will also be some things you haven't heard or read anywhere else before. In a program dealing with people in career transitions, the author Mark Stein asked, "Who can resist the temptation to blame one's shortcomings on some childhood trauma, whether real or imagined?" And then he proposed, "It's true you are the way you are because of your past, but staying that way is an active decision."

It's now time that I share a secret with you: I will bring no value to you in this book. This book isn't worth anything on its own. Only you can make it worth something. Only you can create the value from what I've written here. How? You create value for yourself by taking the actions necessary to produce the life you want to have. *Don't wait to feel a certain way before you take action.* **Your feelings will come from the actions you take.** Self-esteem is built on the actions we take. You may not have control over outside influences, circumstances, or even your feelings, but you do have control over the actions you take and the way you respond to your feelings.

To get what you want, you need to be specific about what you ask for. I once read a personal ad where a lady asked to meet, "A big, strong, vegetarian, animal lover." Do you realize if a gorilla showed up she would have gotten what she asked for? That's probably not what she wanted, but it would have been what she asked for.

I believe strongly in the power of written, I said **written**, **goals**. In 1987, I was having some marital difficulty. Every evening I wrote, "My marital problems will be resolved." Two weeks later my wife came to me and said, "Rennie, I want a divorce."

This isn't want I wanted, but it was what I asked for. Maybe I should have been writing, "Judi and I will have a happy married life." It is too late now but with marriage counseling, it turned out to be the best for both of us. Counseling allowed us to get at what was really in the way of our having a loving marriage, not the things we made up. It allowed us to separate without blaming the other partner. In 1993, six years after Judi and I separated, my second wife, Lesli, and I went up to visit my daughter in Seattle and stayed with my ex-wife and her new husband for two days. This comes from setting and taking actions on our goals. So you see, I've experienced relationships that work, and I think anything is possible.

Even experts can be wrong about what is possible. Look at the following quotes:

"The phonograph has no commercial value." You already know phonographs were a huge commercial success. And guess who said that? How about Thomas Edison in 1880 He ought to know, he invented it—but he was wrong, wasn't he?

"Sensible and responsible women do not want to vote." Would you believe this came from the president of our country in 1905, Grover Cleveland? Was this a guy ahead of his time, or what?

"Who the hell wants to hear actors talk?" Harry Warner of Warner Brothers Studios said this in 1927. This guy was in the movie business, he ought to know—but if it hadn't been for his brother, Jack Warner, they wouldn't have made talkies.

"I think there's a world market for about five computers." Tom Watson, chairman of IBM said this in 1943. I think he was wrong. What do you think?

Ken Olson, the president of DEC computers said this in 1977: *"There is no reason for an individual to have a computer in their home."* Talk about a visionary. This book was written on my home computer. I produced PowerPoint presentations and manage my client & tenant database on a home computer. Maybe Kenny's right and I'm wrong, but I doubt it.

35

Here are some final examples of what "experts" have said:

"We don't like their sound, and guitar music is on the way out."
—Decca Recording Company rejecting the Beatles, 1962

"Heavier-than-air flying machines are impossible."
—Lord Kelvin, president, Royal Society, 1895.

"If I would have thought about it, I wouldn't have done the experiment. The literature was full of examples that said you can't do this."
—Spencer Silver on the work which led to the unique adhesives for 3M Post-it notepads.

I could go on for pages about experts who said such things: "The radio had no commercial value." "Computers could never weigh less than 1.5 tons." "The microchip isn't good for anything." "Data processing is just a fad." "The telephone has no value for communication." And, "No one would pay for overnight delivery, even if it was feasible, which it isn't."

Have experts told you what you can or can't have, or do, or be? Maybe they weren't even experts, but well-meaning relatives or friends. Are you going to limit yourself based on the limited thinking of people who have expressed their negative beliefs in your direction? I am asking you to think for yourself. I was lucky. My mother didn't impose limiting beliefs on me. I think she figured I could do anything I wanted, and my dad didn't live long enough to tell me what I "wasn't" capable of doing.

Because my father died when I was eleven and my mom was a single parent who was not around much, I developed other limiting beliefs on my own. As an example, in my child-mind I figured that if my parents weren't around to take care of me, it must be because I was not worthy of their care. As an adult, I operated on the belief that if my parents wouldn't help me, then no one else would either. I invented a limiting belief and avoided asking for help.

The point is we either invent beliefs that limit us, or limiting beliefs are given to us by people we depend upon or respect. In either case, they are inventions and, as such, we can choose to believe them, discard them, alter them or transform them. Each one of us has the power to choose how we will let our circumstances affect us. I choose not to have them limit me. I choose to go after what I want and you can choose to do the same.

It doesn't work to judge yourself, or other people, based on past circumstances or situations. We all have the ability to create our own future. An example would be a poor black girl born to unwed parents. She was sexually abused from the time she was about age seven and by the time she was fourteen, had a baby which died after a few days. She was thrown out of reform school, her weight bounced all over the place, and she used drugs. While this sounds like a typical talk show guest, I'm describing one of the most successful talk show hosts in the country, Oprah Winfrey. Most people would predict a person coming from this past to amount to nothing. Oprah created her future, and it wasn't based on her past. She said it was reading which saved her. She read about the better life she could have, and she believed it. You can do the same thing.

When it comes to getting what you want, don't bother listening to the people who you think may know more. I'm telling you, when it comes to knowing what you want, you know best!

Step 2.

Plan your future, S.M.A.R.T. Goals

How to set long term goals and the action steps to achieve them

The key to setting financial goals is to be specific. Effective goals need to be SMART. I don't mean smart like my mouth. Smart is an acronym for Specific, Measurable, Action-oriented, Realistic and Time-limited.

Specific
Goals need to be specific. As an example, I could say, "I want people to like me," when what I mean is that I want Dianne to like me. Well, how will I know if she likes me?

Measurable
If I ask Dianne to go out to a play and she accepts, I say she likes me; I create the measurement. If you said you wanted more money and I gave you a penny, you'd have more money. Instead, you could have said, "I want $1,000." Then we'd have something to measure to see if you got what you asked for. You create the measurement.

Action-oriented

This means the goal is not static. It involves doing something. Do not use the words going to. That's like saying, "I'm going to be rich." You are always going there, but never arrive. Use verbs like living, sailing, flying, driving, cruising, and so on.

Realistic

I can't say what's realistic for anybody. There used to be a program on TV called "Mystery Science Theater 3000." It was on the Comedy Cable Channel about a guy that's trapped in space and forced to watch the worst movies ever made. The creator of the show and his two robots talked over the soundtrack and made funny comments throughout the movie. He was told when he was in high school that he watched too much television. His teacher said, "You can't earn a living watching TV." Guess what? He earned a living watching TV.

Barry Bonds, baseball's home run champion, was told by his high school science teacher that he could not earn a living playing baseball, so he better buckle down and study his text books. Barry Bonds has made history, but not his high school teacher. So I'm in no position to say what's realistic or what's fantasy for someone else. That's something you have to decide for yourself.

Time-limited

A goal is nothing more than a dream that's got a time deadline attached to it.

Let's tie together two parts of SMART goals: Specific and Time. In my workshops, I often ask this question, "Do you want to be rich?" Many people raise their hand indicating they want to be rich. Would you? Then I single out several people who raised their hand and ask, "How much is 'rich?'" Guess what? Hardly anyone is able to tell me how much money is "rich." They're probably rich now and don't know it.

You may be in the same category. You have a place to live, food to eat. That's better than millions of people on this planet. Any book you want to read, you can go to the library and read it for free. Anywhere you want to travel in this country, they've paved the roads for you, and you rarely have to pay any tolls. I'd say you're rich now.

But let's talk numbers: $100,000, $1 million, $3 million, $5 million, $100 million. It doesn't really matter. We just need something *specific* so we can talk about *time*.

Let's say your reply is, "$5 million would be rich." Now, when do you want to be rich? If you say "now," you weren't paying attention. Remember when I was talking about realistic versus fantasy? That's where this would fit, unrealistic.

I can't say for sure, though. Maybe you're on the edge of a huge income breakthrough. You're up for the starring role in some movie, or your script is about to be purchased for a princely sum, or you've got a winning lottery ticket. I don't know.

Instead of saying you want to be rich "now," let's say you picked ten years. This is how you break it down: If you created or accumulated about $345,000 per year at 8%, you'd have the $5 million in ten years. (Note: $345,000 in ten years is only $3,450,000 in deposits. The other $465,000 is interest earnings.)

Next, you want to have the goal written in present tense, from the future, as in the following example:

It is June 15, 2019 and I am excited as I relax on the beach in Hawaii and check my laptop to see another monthly deposit of $50,000 in rents to my checking account. (This would be written in 2014.)

You also need to include how you will *feel*. This is one of the reasons *why* you want to achieve the goal. This is one of the most overlooked important ingredients in goal setting. It's in a few books, tapes and programs, but not all.

Think for a moment. Can you tell me something you do that does not include how you feel? You could be so disconnected from your feelings you may not even be sure what I've just asked. As an example: How do you feel when you drive to work? Happy, sad, resentful, scared, numb, joyous? *Why* are you doing this activity? How do you *feel*?

There are only two reasons why we do anything: We want to either avoid pain or we want to gain pleasure. Development of this theory goes back to Sigmund Freud, Pavlov and others, and has been popularized by Tony Robbins and N.L.P. (Neuro Linguistic Programming). (You can learn more about N.L.P. in the appendix.) Can you think of anything else you do that doesn't involve either avoiding pain or seeking pleasure? Probably not.

So, if those are the only things that are motivating people, avoiding pain or gaining pleasure, you need to include the feelings you want to have in your goal. That's the only reason you're doing it. That's the "why" you want it. That must be clear for you, because that's what is going to motivate you.

Do you want $5 million so you can feel relaxed and retire on a yacht? Feel a sense of accomplishment because you can feed the hungry of the world? Feel confident, able, free, joyous, or secure? Do you want $5 million to feel abandoned, ashamed, baffled, confused, defeated, embarrassed, empty, humble, insecure, jealous, panicky, righteous, spiteful, tense or unloved? Or, do you want $5 million to feel worshipped? Or, do you figure it will make you feel the opposite of those feelings? (Check the appendix for a large list of feeling words.)

Get clear on *why*. The clarity of the why creates the power to take action.

The two most overlooked keys to achieving your goals

I'm now going to tell you about the other two most commonly overlooked elements in achieving your goals: other people and tracking results.

1. *Other people*
It's vital to have other people involved. Share it with other people. Do not work on it by yourself. Have other people support you. Get outside advice and coaching. Find a mentor. Model

someone you respect, get them to assist you. Are you picking up a theme here? You don't need other people . . . any more than you need a stove to cook food. You could use a campfire, barbecue or fireplace. It just makes life easier and more rewarding.

Achieving goals is something you do with other people. It is not done by yourself. We can all learn something from Alcoholics Anonymous: When there was just one drunk who wanted to stay sober, he found someone else. In trying to keep other people from dying of alcohol abuse, he stayed sober. If working together can keep people from killing themselves from drinking, do you think it might also work with something as simple as achieving your goals?

I am suggesting it's doubtful you'll do anything of consequence by yourself. Lee Iacocca did not turn around Chrysler by himself in 1979. Who did he have help from? Everybody: The Federal government, taxpayers, stockholders, executives, unions, managers, supervisors, and line workers. Practically everybody. He did not turn Chrysler around by himself.

If there is a goal you want to accomplish, if you ignore everything I have said about effective goals up to this point, and all you do is work with other people, you've got a 90% likelihood of achieving it. Why? Because the people with whom you are working will help you focus on making your goal specific and measurable. They'll question you about being realistic and having a time deadline. They will support you in getting what you want.

In 1994, I took a workshop because I had a desire to work four days a week instead of seven (using other people's definition of work). My son had a great definition of work. He says, "It's only work if you'd rather be doing something else."

Anyway, I said I wanted to limit my work to four days per week. Someone in my group asked me what I wanted to do on the other three days. I had no answer. I didn't have a why like I said you needed. The only things that came to mind were writing, reading and going to workshops—things I already did whenever I wanted to. It took talking with someone else to get clear on what I wanted. It's other people who can help you get what you want, or get clear on what you want.

Are you afraid that if you ask other people for help, they're going to tell you to drop dead or something? If you ask other people for assistance, they will want to help you. If you ask ten people for directions, eight of them will be thrilled to help. All you have to do is ask. If someone asked you for support, you'd provide it if you could. Wouldn't you?

Back when I was doing personal financial coaching, about 70% of my clients were women, and very few of them had a problem asking for help. The comments you've read are directed primarily to men. Do you know why Moses was lost in the desert for 40 years on a trip that should have taken 4 weeks? He wouldn't ask for directions. (I guess it's a macho thing passed down for generations.)

It's possible you could achieve what you want by yourself, but it's only a 10% possibility. If you involve other people and let them assist you, you've got a 90% likelihood of success. James Prochaska, a University of Rhode Island professor, has conducted several studies on the effectiveness of support groups. In his book *Changing for the Good*, he says 90-95% of the people who try to modify their behavior on their own - without the support of a group or professional counseling - fail. It you were a gambler, which odds would you prefer? 1). Ask others for support or help: 90% success rate. 2). Do it by yourself: 10% success rate. I suggest you let others support you. All you have to do is ask. The following are two ways to work with other people; coaching and speaking to others.

Speak to others and ask for coaching

It's funny if you think about this: Why is it the finest athletes in the world have a coach? Is it because they're incompetent, helpless, don't know what they're doing or how to do it effectively? Of course not. They have a coach because they recognize the value of having someone hold them to account, or hold them to a higher standard than they've yet to achieve. I guess regular people don't need coaches, though. It makes more sense for regular people to continue to make mistakes and get no feedback. Right? Repeating what doesn't work builds character. Obviously, these are silly comments, but they illustrate the silly thinking we sometimes have, like, "I want to prove I can do it all by myself with no help from anyone."

A coach doesn't always tell you something new. Sometimes they tell you something you already knew, but a little differently or at the time you most needed to hear it. They can create the opportunity for you to have a shift in attitude about what you thought you could accomplish. They can hold you to account to do another 2%, which when repeated over and over again results in a huge shift in what you were previously doing.

Even though I'm semi-retired, I still coach four to six business owners or professionals in a year. It is such a joy to work with people who can take the coaching and produce results. A recent client in the construction business is such an example. I would suggest he take a vacation with his family, or sell a piece of property, or set up a meeting with a particular person and he would just do it. In the six months we worked together, his net worth increased from $900,000 to $1.5 million. That's a $600,000 increase in six months. He said the $3,000 fee was well worth it.

Coaching is designed to empower you to use more of the talent you already have, to apply more of your skills and abilities, to break up the limiting thinking which may hold you back from applying those skills and talents, to support you in making choices which can alter the quality of your life. If you look at it, the quality of your life comes down to the decisions you make on a moment-by-moment, day-by-day basis. Haven't there been decisions you've made that have changed your life, both for the positive as well as the negative? Haven't there been decisions you've made which were colored by the understanding you had at the time about a particular situation or person, and they shifted what could have been the result in either a good or bad way? Of course you have.

A cat may not know the results of walking on a hot stove, but once it burns its paws it will make better decisions in the future. Like the cat, many of us have learned through pain. We tried things and may have used poor judgment, which gave us information about what doesn't work. As a result, we may look at how we can make a better decision next time, or we may react to and avoid anything that looks like the same situation. The word *distinctions* is used to describe this concept of using information to make different decisions. The research I've done indicates several authorities who offer transformation programs use this concept, including Anthony Robbins and Werner Erhard, the founder of EST.

A 'distinction' is defined in the dictionary as quality or characteristic that makes something different. Someone might give us a flower, and we will make that mean something. What happened is; we were given a flower. What it means or the interpretation is what we add to it—such as the person likes us, wants something from us, or is just weird. The distinction is that the two events are separate and different; receiving the flower and the meaning we assign to it. However, in our normal day-to-day life we combine the two events into one and cannot distinguish one from the other. The cat does not recognize what must occur for the stove to be hot. It only knows it must stay away after it is burned. We have the ability to see the difference between a hot stove and one that is cool.

To produce the financial results available to you, you will want to see the difference between how you've taken actions in the past and results. Just be aware that it is difficult to be open to a more powerful and fulfilling life if you refuse to look at the interpretation or meaning you have assigned to a past event. If you've shared something personal with someone who later used that to hurt you, it could mean you should never share anything personal again. Or, it could mean you need to be more discerning about with whom you share personal information. A coaching relationship can provide the clarity and distinctions you may be looking for.

This book is like a coach. This book is my attempt to reach out and provide you with information you may already know but not be using, to dig a little deeper when you hear something negative from another, to provide the motivation for you to use what you know. I may provide some new information, and I hope I provide the inspiration for you to take action on it. I will provide tools to create financial independence which you may or may not have had before, but explain it in a way that creates a desire for you to use the tools and create prosperity for yourself. And, the most powerful way to create or produce the results you want is to go beyond this book and work with other people. This book cannot interrupt your faulty thinking; that requires another person. But two people can use this book as a guide to coach one another.

Another way to evaluate a choice, besides our own experience, is to use the experience of others. You will find the experience of others in this book. We don't have to get beat up as we learn things if we're willing to see what worked, or didn't work, for others. The key is to determine how similar you are to the frame of reference you're using.

Because your uncle, aunt, whoever, went broke in a grocery business or lost money in the stock market doesn't mean the same will happen to you. Speak to them or others who knew them and get the whole picture. I recall a story one of my clients told me about a grandfather who went broke in the depression and lost his business, as if the depression was the cause. When he investigated further by speaking with his aunt and uncle he discovered this grandfather was an alcoholic and a gambler. He would have destroyed any business regardless of what was going on in the economy.

People say things like "Stocks are bad" because they lost money. What they don't tell you is they were gambling in "penny stocks" and not investing in well-respected or profitable corporations such as General Electric, 3M, Coca-Cola, Microsoft or Walmart. You have to get more information as to why they say what they say before you take it at face value. How similar are your knowledge, skills, and attitudes to theirs?

If, after all I've provided so far, you're still reluctant to ask other people to help you, I need to ask you this, "What makes you so grand, noble and regal to rip off other people of the good feelings they could have?" I assert the following: When you don't ask other people for assistance or allow them to support you, you're ripping them off. You're taking away from them the opportunity to feel good about themselves, by contributing to you. I hope you can hear what I'm saying because this is the most important key to getting what you want.

I'm sure you know there are some people not to ask. Right? You know who they are. They're the family members who tell you that you're an idiot for thinking you deserve what you're asking for. They're the co-workers who have their lives in the toilet, and want to tell you why you belong in there with them. Use your head—either stay away from these people or, if you're inclined, pull them out of the toilet.

2. *Tracking Results*

The second vital missing component in most goal setting workshops involves tracking your results. (The first was working with other people.) It's taking the time to write down the small daily action steps and milestones in the calendar you use, appointment book, iPhone, computer, or Week At-A-Glance. Whatever it is you use, you need to write your action steps in there and monitor how you're doing compared to what you planned.

Are you aware how much of the time a plane flying between Los Angeles and New York is "off course?" It's about 95% of the time. How can that be? It's simple. The plane follows a type of radar tracking beam. When it gets off course to the north a few degrees the instruments alert the flight crew, then they correct to the south. They pass right by the beam again and when they get too far to the south, they're alerted again and correct. They do this hundreds of times during the flight. In addition, they communicate with air traffic controllers. (Look what showed up: pilots not producing the goal by themselves!) If they weren't paying attention, or didn't have this beam to guide them, they could end up in Miami instead of New York.

When I was working on one of my goals, which was writing my first book, I wrote in my appointment book how many chapters I had to have completed by a certain date. When I got to that date in my appointment book, if I wasn't where I needed to be with the number of chapters, I knew I was off track. I could take some corrective action. If I didn't have the guideposts written in my appointment book, I could have just wandered farther and farther off track.

The Five-Year Financial Goal

This could be considered the first tool to creating anything you want. But, it's so big and important it's like the box that holds all the tools. While we will be focusing on financial issues, please recognize the power of this toolbox. It's not that it's a five-year goal: it could be one year, ten years or one hundred years. It's not even required to be a goal. It could be an objective, mission or vision. The power is in writing it down.

There is a powerful way to write your five-year goal that is more effective than any other method I've researched, studied, tested or used. There are two basic ways you can do it: You could start thinking about a five-year goal by saying to yourself, "Here is where I am today. And, based on where I am today, this is where it looks like I'll be in five years." That's one way of doing it.

That's *not* the way I'm going to ask you to do it. That's writing a goal in the present and figuring out what it's going to look like in five years. I gave you a correct example about 10 pages ago. The process I'm recommending comes from Barbara Sher's book, *Wishcraft*. What I want you to do is make believe you've got a magic wand. (Pick up a pencil or pen and wave it around. Stop worrying if you look silly or not. Wave it like it has magic, because it does.) Wave that wand like you can have anything you want.

49

What I want you to do now is divorce yourself from the present. I want you to stand in the future of what you want and write a goal based on what you want. This is the most important concept to grasp: Pick the future you want from the future, not the present. This is to be a goal not connected to or built from where you are today, but based on the future you want to have.

This is how I wrote my goal in 1994:

It is January 27, 1999. I am thrilled and happy being interviewed on *Good Morning America* about my book *Wealth on Any Income*. Through my company, The Financial Coach, I am a nationally known and respected speaker and consultant on the issues of people's feelings and attitudes about money. My workshops, materials, tapes and books have helped thousands of people handle their money more effectively.

Let's examine the components of this goal.

"It is January 27, 1999." Was that the date at the time? No, I said write it in present tense and stand in the future. Mine was five years in the future when I wrote it in 1994.

"I am thrilled and happy being interviewed (here are the feelings and the action) on *Good Morning America* about my book *Wealth on Any Income*." When I show up on this show, will you be able to measure if this happened? It's specific, isn't it?

"Through my company, The Financial Coach, I am considered a nationally known and respected speaker and consultant on the issues of people's feelings and attitudes about money. My workshops, materials, tapes and books have helped thousands of people handle their money more effectively." That's what I wrote.

I only had three handicaps when I wrote the above goal. The first handicap was I didn't know how to write well; second, I didn't know how to write a book; and third, I didn't even know anyone who knew how to write a book.

Would it have made any sense to write this goal if I stood in the present and looked at where I was? No. Instead, I stepped into the future and I wrote a goal based on what I wanted! And, guess what? The handicaps got solved.

I shared the goal with my ex-wife. I said, "I want to have a book out, but I don't know how to write a book."

She responded, "Why don't you talk to Steve?" This is her brother, my ex-brother-in-law. I forgot he was an author! Have you heard of Prentice-Hall, the big publishing company? That's who published his books. And, guess what? There were only four authors with that company that generated more in book revenues than he did. He was their fifth largest, income-producing author, with a seven-figure annual income. The guy knows how to write books, and it's my own ex-brother-in-law. So I called him up and said, "Will you show me?" and he said, "Of course."

I went to his home in Del Mar and I found out the mechanics of how to write a book. Now, the only problem was, I didn't know how to write.

Next, as a member of an apartment owners association, I was given the opportunity to write some articles for their magazine. I didn't think I knew how to write, but because I continued to share with people what I wanted, I met someone who was writing for a newspaper, Mischa Martin. I asked her (again, help from other people) if she would read my article and give me some feedback. And she said, "Sure."

We got together over lunch one day. She was looking over my article and asked if it was okay to make some corrections. I said that would be fine. She showed me how I had the present tense and the past tense in the same paragraph. She corrected the grammar. She asked me what I meant to say with some sentences. With her red pen, she cleaned up the whole thing. When she handed it back to me, it looked liked it bled to death, so I commented, "Boy, I knew I didn't know how to write."

She said, "You write beautifully, what are you talking about?"

I responded, "What do you mean? Look at all these corrections you made."

She looked at me kind of puzzled and said, "I just did what an editor would do."

I blurted, "Oh! You mean that's not the same as writing?" She replied, "No, writers write. Editors edit."

I've never forgotten that, and I would have never learned it unless I had written a goal from the future, not the present.

Something else I learned: I can be an author, and not even write down one word. Do you think Lee Iacocca or Jerry West wrote their own autobiographies? I can tell you they didn't. They were just the authors. A writer was hired who physically sat down and wrote the book.

Your Five-Year Financial Goal

Now it's your turn. I want you to take five minutes to write either a financial or a career goal that describes what you want five years in the future, written from the future. If you take any more than five minutes, then you may be filtering out what you think you can have. Stop reading now and write down what you want as a five-year career or financial goal. Don't wait to do this until the right time. The right time is right now.

It is _____ (date).
I am _____ (feelings)
(action verbs) _____.

Did you stop and write? Come on! This is for you. If you were in one of my workshops you couldn't get away without writing a five year goal. Everyone else around you would be writing while you were staring into space. I've got what I want. It's time for you to work on getting what you want. By the way, if you have some conversation in your head about what you deserve, or don't deserve, drop it! Just write what you want, please.

You cannot do the next step unless you've written your five-year goal.

For the next step, you can either work backwards to figure out where you need to be at 2 years, 1 year, 6 months, and so on. Or, you can jump to what needs to be done tomorrow.

It is _____

Again, this process came from the book *Wishcraft* by Barbara Sher. It's one of the best books I've read on how to get what you want and is listed in the resource section. Barbara was a therapist in New York and did workshops all over the country for the Learning Annex. When I attended one of her workshops she made a suggestion to me that sped up by years the attainment of my goals.

To figure out what you can do tomorrow, create a list of all of the items you can imagine which need to be done to achieve your goal. Look over your list and ask yourself the question, "Can I do this tomorrow?"

It seems like every goal I've seen had the same first step. It was *research*. Research is going to google, a library, bookstore, magazine stand, or talking to someone who might have some information.

As an example, let's say you want to be a doctor in five years. Tomorrow you could talk to a doctor to find out what to do first. You could call up and ask, "What do I do to get started? What do you suggest? What do you recommend? Who else can I talk to?" You could go up to a librarian and ask for books to research. You could call a medical school and ask for some advice.

If you want to have an international business you could call the chamber of commerce, go to the library, or ask someone you know if they know someone who has an international business. Key point: When you ask someone for assistance and they don't have the information or knowledge on your subject, ask them who they know who might know, and contact that person.

The Action Structure to Produce Results

What you are now beginning to create I call the ***Action Structure to Produce Results.*** You're writing down what you want. You're writing the timeframe for completing certain milestones, you're figuring out what you have to do to get started, and you're going to be talking to people who can assist you.

Now you must write down *specifically* what you will do tomorrow. Let me repeat that. You must write down specifically what you will do tomorrow. You must write down who you will talk to, where you will go, and what time of day you will do what's needed. This is where your appointment book comes into play, or calendar, iPhone or whatever you use to remind yourself of what needs to be done. If you don't have one, go buy one, that's your first step. Go out tomorrow and get an appointment book or daily planner. The structure that produces results comes from writing down what you need to do and placing it where you will see it so you can act on it.

Also, today or tomorrow, find the people, or person who will be willing to hold you accountable for doing what needs to be done to get what you want. Remember, you don't do this stuff by yourself. Where do you find this person? Ask a friend, relative, co-worker, or neighbor. Join a 12-step program, church, temple, or support group. Form your own if you can't find one. Bring together people who want to change their lives and use this book as a guide to getting started.

Tomorrow I will _____ at _____ (time of day).

Remember, write it down where you will see it and take action on it. Tell others what you are going to do and ask them to check with you to see if you did it. Set up a specific date and time to speak with them. You could earn a living as a "life coach" just by following this structure.

The resource section in the back of the book lists various books, tapes, meetings, magazines, newsletters and organizations that you can use for support in achieving the goals you desire. The concept behind the list is even more important than the concept of the list.

Let me illustrate the concept by asking you the following:

Did you eat yesterday?

Did you eat again today, or plan to?

Yes? Oh! What was wrong with what you ate yesterday?

Is there something wrong with you that you need to eat everyday?

Do these seem like dumb questions?

Of course, there's nothing wrong with what you ate, how you ate, or who you are. It's natural to eat every day. Your body uses up the food and you eat again. This is natural and normal.

Let's try some other questions:

Did you bathe yesterday?

Did you bathe today?

Do you figure you're probably going to bathe again tomorrow?

If you answered yes, does this mean there is something wrong with the way you bathe?

Could there be something wrong with you?

Gee, maybe this is natural, too. Is it possible this is normal, too? Your body gets dirty and you have to wash it again if you want to be socially acceptable.

Okay, I know I'm going to get you on this one. Do you feel inspired to take action on your financial goals because of reading this book? If you've read this far I would expect your answer to be yes. Have you ever been to a workshop, or read a book, or listened to a sermon or tape program and afterwards felt motivated to take some action? Did that enthusiasm wear off after a few days? Did you ever wonder if there was something wrong with the message you got, the person who delivered it or something wrong with you when it wore off after a few days? Lots of people say they felt this, or thought this.

I don't get it. What produces more results, your body or your mind? Your mind. Right? It's the mind that produces the results, and you feed and bathe your body every day, and it wears off, and that is normal. When motivation wears off, why do you act like something's wrong? How come you're not rushing to read another book, or listen to another tape or CD, or pick up the phone and talk to someone who can support you? This is called feeding your mind. If this is what *you* do, congratulations! If this isn't what you do, how come you're not feeding your mind again? Isn't that what's missing? When you're not motivated or inspired anymore it means your mind is hungry. So feed it.

That's why the resource list is so important as a concept. It lists food for your head. It's natural for the motivation to wear off, just like it's natural for the food to wear off. It doesn't mean there's anything wrong with what you heard or who said it. It doesn't mean there's anything wrong with you. It's natural that it wears off; it means your mind is hungry and you need to feed it.

Just like your body needs food, it also needs exercise. If you went to the gym and lifted weights once, would you expect that to last you for the rest of your life? No? Then why would you expect to attend a financial planning workshop and expect to be inspired for life?

It seems as though many people think, "Oh, golly, I guess there's something wrong with me." It would be like thinking, "I showed up to the gym once and lifted some weights and figured now I'm fit." Or, "I went to a workshop once and got inspired, but it wore off, so there's no point going again. I figure it ought to last for two years." That's stupid, isn't it?

Our drive, motivation and inspiration will wear off just like the food we eat. We all need to continue to feed our minds because that's what produces the results. With awareness, tools and actions, you can create financial prosperity and financial freedom. After you complete the next two sections, I invite you to write to me and tell me how successful you've been using this program. I'd love to hear from you. Now, let's address some challenges and solve them.

How the Problem Started

You're not alone and it's not your fault. Remember the questions I asked about where you learned how to handle money? Wherever I ask those questions, the results are the same. Whether it's in my public workshops or corporate training, when I address a conference of accountants or financial planners, or even when I train high school teachers, the answer is the same: Less than 8% of the people were given instructions early in life on how to handle money. That means while we are all expected to know how to handle money, 92% of us have not been taught. This is why I say it's not your fault.

The grand essentials to happiness in this life are something to do, someone to love, and something to hope for.
—Joseph Addison

Step 3.

Recognize Good Debt from Bad Debt

Bad Debt

How did this problem (or challenge) of so many people having nothing after 40 years of work begin? We've already seen how you've not been taught in school or by your parents to handle money effectively. So, maybe the banks can help. Do you remember when you opened your first checking account how the new accounts person showed you how to balance it? No?

How about when you got your first credit card? Didn't the bank explain how to use it wisely? Didn't they warn you not to abuse it? Didn't they tell you debt was easier to get into than out of? You don't remember that? Probably because it never happened.

Maybe under hypnosis we can create a memory for you, and you can make believe you were told those things and then feel guilty because you think you're too stupid to do what they said. Not likely. Of the thousands of people I've spoken to, fewer than 10% were given any kind of financial education.

It's more likely you get items in the mail encouraging you to abuse your credit card, with suggestions such as buying your groceries, getting frequent flyer miles and discounts on a new car. Or touting contests in which each charge becomes a game entry with only one winner. Bank of America ran a contest like this in 1995. Each time someone used their card, it was another entry into the contest and the winner got their balance paid in full. Well, what about everyone else? What about the tens of thousands who ran up their credit limits? You know who got stuck paying that off, don't you?

The people I met in my workshops and those who bought my materials were all smart enough to know how to balance a checkbook and understand the risks of debt when it was explained to them. Anyway, who says you have to personally balance your checking account? I don't do mine. My bookkeeper can do it better and three times faster than me. So, she does it. I just write down what she needs. If you don't want to do it, you can find someone else to do it. I'm just suggesting you get it done.

An inability to handle debt is one of the major roadblocks to creating financial freedom. So, how did this problem of credit abuse start? In the early 60s credit cards came into common use with the Bank of America Visa cards as one of the pioneers. As I said, no instructions were provided, no warnings other than small print, and using credit was glamorized.

Let's say you just left home to start out on your own or just got married or re-married. You want to furnish an apartment and you go shopping at various department stores. It doesn't matter which one, because the way they finance merchandise is very similar. The following is an example for a furniture sale from a department store advertisement. You're a smart shopper and wait until furniture is on sale before you buy. You pick out a dining set with a retail sale price of $599, and with the sales tax it totals $648. The advertisement offers the opportunity to pay only **$12 A Month***. Now you tell me which is more attractive, **$648** or $12 per month? The * next to the monthly payment in the advertisement directs you to the finance charges.

Make believe department stores are charitable organizations and they decided not to charge interest. How long would it take to pay off the furniture at $12 per month? Most people don't take the few moments necessary to figure this out. It would be 54 months, or 4.5 years. However, this is *without interest*. Department stores are not charitable institutions; they are businesses. Just like any other business they have to pay rent, utilities, salaries, and shipping fees whether someone comes in and buys something or not. They deserve to make a profit. If businesses don't make a profit they couldn't stay open, and then you would have nowhere to purchase furniture, groceries or anything else.

Well, they do charge interest; **21.6%** in California. It varies from state to state, but that's the rate in most states. The others range from 18–21%. Generally, most department stores— Macy's, Sears, JCPenney, and even K-Mart—are at that same level or higher. It's easy to see, if you carry a balance and pay over an extended period of time, you would pay less interest with a Visa or MasterCard than using a department store card.

Adding in the interest, your payments will last a little longer. Want to guess how much longer? Do you think it would go from 4.5 years to 7 or 10 years? *Wrong!* At 21.6% interest your payments would stretch out for more than *17 years!* At $12 per month, if you had a four-year-old child they could be done with college before you paid off the furniture, providing the furniture lasted that long. Your $12 per month payments for 205 months totals $2, 460.

With a sale price of $600, if you purchased it on credit you would have paid $2,460. That's about *400% of retail!* (2,460 ÷ 600 = 4 times retail).

Have you heard of the book *Buying Retail Is Stupid* by King, Newmark and Cunningham? In that book, they list stores all over California where you can "get it wholesale." So, let me ask you—if paying retail is stupid, what is it when you pay 400% of retail?

If we look at finance charges from another angle, it would be the additional profit the store earns. If most stores purchase merchandise for half of what they sell it for, then our $600 dining set costs the store $300. Again, the profit is used to pay rent, salaries, utilities and more, and there's no guarantee they will sell each item they buy. When you pay for an item in full, whether you pay cash or write a check, the store will have a 100% gross profit, or $300 in my example. However, if you finance the purchase as I've shown, the store would have a *profit of $2,160.* This is an increase in *profit to 720%.* Now, you tell me: Does a store want you to buy something and pay in full, or finance it? That's right, they don't care what you buy, as long as you finance it. The profit is in financing, not retail sales. If you don't believe me, look at the annual report of Sears, or any other public department store.

If you're carrying a balance on your credit cards and you make minimum payments, you could be paying 180-400% for whatever you purchased. Actually, if you allow the payment to reduce as the balance declines, which is the way minimum payments work, you could pay even more. If you saw an item you wanted on sale for 25% less, and you didn't have the money to buy it right then, don't put it on a credit card and make minimum payments. You would be better off to save up and pay the full price. Full price would only be 100% of retail. Paying it off on time even at the reduced price would be 150% or more of retail.

Think about it. You go out for dinner and spend $30, and charge it. First, you just spent plenty for someone else to prepare the food. Second, by the next morning your body has processed it and you dispose of the waste. Third, if you have a balance on your card and you make a minimum payment, you'll now spend 15 or 20 months paying for the meal you disposed of the next morning. Does this make sense to you?

What are the attitudes that caused this mess? First, many people viewed their credit limit as an increase in income. *It's not income, it's debt.*

Second, Madison Avenue is not your ally in creating financial independence. Advertisers do not want you to keep your money; they want you to spend it. And, they're going to tell you how. They want you to be their pawn. There are plenty of people who want to live well off your money. There's a reason the United

States is a *consumer* society. Advertisers want you to consume. The definition of the word consume is to *use up, waste, squander, destroy totally and ravage.* This is how Madison Avenue advertisers view you. Not as a consumer, but as someone who wastes, squanders and destroys.

I'm not one to propose conspiracy theories. In a short article in the Los Angeles Times on October 22, 1996, it was reported that John L. Mitchell and Sam Fullwood III had done research into American politics and history. They concluded that people who feel powerless in society also suspect that grand forces control their lives. It leads to the type of violent actions taken by the Ku Klux Klan or those responsible for the Oklahoma City bombing. Those who feel they have some power in their own lives give greater credence to the role of the individuals shaping both history and their own destiny. This lead to the kinds of actions taken by Ghandi in having the British leave India, Martin Luther King, Jr. moving our nation to a greater level of equality, or Golda Meir becoming one of the first women leaders of a nation. You have to choose for yourself whether you feel you have the ability to alter your own circumstances or your life is controlled and dominated by grand forces. Beware of the methods used to market consumer goods, services, and even money. Despite what you hear in an advertisement, you still have the power to choose to buy or not buy, to believe what you are told or not to believe it.

When you look at what your neighbors are doing, your extended family members, the people you work with, or even the people you go to for advice, you'll see they've bought into a system that will have them be wage slaves for the rest of their lives. They've been sold the idea then can buy now and pay later. They can have any car they want, furniture, clothing, vacations, or homes on low easy monthly payments. You're even encouraged to use a credit card to charge meals in a restaurant and groceries at the store. Discover calls it 'Smart Money.' How is it smart to pay 200% to 300% of retail?

If you look closely, you'll see that most people handle money in a way that obligates them to make payments to finance companies, department stores, or other creditors for the rest of their lives, and they think there's no way off the treadmill or, worse yet, this is the way to live the good life. They're trapped in their job or career because of the monthly payments that have to be made month in and month out, year in and year out. Retirement is unrealistic. And, my talking about financial independence is not only a dream, it's a cruel joke. Stop listening to people who have bought into a system that is designed to have you work the rest of your life for financial institutions. It doesn't have to be that way, and I'll show you how to end the cycle of debt and create financial independence.

Dahlstrom & Company did a survey to find out the top three recreational activities for people in the United States. Do you know the game "Family Feud" where 100 people surveyed provide the answers? I think that's how this survey was conducted. The number three recreational activity was "shopping." The number two activity was "watch TV." And, the number one recreational activity was "do nothing." Please don't ask me how this is done. I haven't met anyone who knows. I can just imagine myself saying, "Honey, I'm done watching TV. I think I'll go do nothing now."

Well, if you're involved in the number two activity, watching TV, what do you see every 10–15 minutes? Commercials to encourage you to go out and buy something, whereby you partake in the number three leading activity, "shopping." Or, let's say you watch the Home Shopping Network. You can do the recreational activities "TV" and "shopping" at the same time; telephone in one hand and credit card in the other. Would you define this as a fulfilling life? I hope not.

Finally, even the credit issuers abuse our language and twist it to induce you to finance everything you purchase. On November 11, 1996, the Los Angeles Times reported GE Credit was going to tack on a $25 fee to people who pay off their balances promptly. In the article, it states the credit industry considers these people "freeloaders" or "deadbeats." Can you imagine that? If you handle money responsibly by paying off your balance each month, you're considered a freeloader or deadbeat.

Take into consideration, whether you pay interest or not, every time you use a credit card the merchant is charged a fee, but apparently that's not enough. If this is how the credit industry views you, then your goal should be to be a freeloader and a deadbeat. This is how advertisers and credit issuers twist the language to influence you to do what is in their best interest, not in your best interest.

A cartoon called "Real Life Adventures" by Wise and Aldrich shows someone reading his mail. He received a letter from a credit issuer that is translated to read as follows:

Congratulations! Because you have no discipline, and are the kind of person who runs up charges and then spends the rest of your life making the minimum payment at usurious interest rates without so much as a peep complaint, and are gullible enough to think this computer-generated fawning letter somehow elevates your status as a person, you've been *pre-approved* for the Garlanbank bronze rewards card!

This is another reason for the credit card mess. It's the opportunity to hide our low self-esteem. This was one of the areas where I saw myself. Let's say I realized I needed some help with budgeting, so I go to the bookstore and I find a helpful book for $3. I open my wallet to find I only have $2. So, I return to the shelf and see what other books could help. I then walk back to the register and charge $30 worth of books to avoid the embarrassment of trying to charge $3.

Some people need to look like a big shot, and that's how they create credit card debt. Again, this deals with low self-esteem. In the early 1980s, my father-in-law and his wife would invite us out to dinner and pay on his credit card. At the time my wife would turn to me and ask, "Do you think my dad can afford this?" I would offer to pay but he wouldn't accept it. We didn't think he could afford it and we were right. When he died, his wife sold off everything, including their home, and she was still left with $25,000 of debts! Then she had to go move in with one of her other children. Is this any way for someone to live in their golden years?

If you're dealing with credit problems, you're not alone. 120 million Americans have credit cards. On the average, they have 10 cards each. Seven out of ten people (72%) carry a balance from one month to the next. I'm telling you that about one out of four people who charge something on their credit card cay pay the balance in full when the statement arrives. One in six pays late, has missed a payment or exceeded their limit. One in ten, or 12 million people, can only make the minimum payment. More than 6 million people can't even make their minimum payments. We're talking about a payment of 2–3% of the balance owed. One in twenty can't even do that. This book will allow you to get off the hamster wheel of credit card use. If you want financial freedom, this is one of the first areas to change your habits, and I'll show you how.

Good Debt

Be aware, not all debt is bad. When someone deposits money in the bank, they are loaning money to the bank. The bank uses the money they've borrowed to make a loan to someone else. The bank is using good debt. They've borrowed at one rate to turn around and make a loan at a higher rate (spread). They make money on the difference in rates. They did not borrow the money to purchase some consumer item or a meal which the next day will turn into . . . well, you know. The bank borrowed money to make money. This is called good debt. Don't get carried away; buying stocks on margin, or borrowing on your home to go into business may or may not be good debt for you. I borrow money to buy apartment buildings. This is good debt.

Depositor loans money to Bank
   (Bank adds spread)
   Bank loans money to Borrower

Excessive debt comes from wanting—and deciding to get everything—*now!* Debt obligates your future income, it's expensive, and the interest payments work against you. It easily leads to overspending. You have probably experienced getting into debt is much easier than getting out of debt.

Knowing Your Credit Score

It's no secret that maintaining good credit is valuable. What you may be unaware of is how many organizations access and use your credit information to make decisions. In addition to those you would expect to check on you like a credit card issuer, department store, mortgage lender or car dealer, it can be a new employer, life or auto insurance company or prospective landlord. Why would a life or auto insurance company care about your credit score, especially if you're not financing anything with them? Some companies feel if you're responsible in how you handle your credit, you will be responsible in how you live your life and drive your car. An employer can expect that if you pay your credit cards on time, you may show up for work on time and also be responsible there. From these situations, you can understand how much others see your good credit as a reflection of who you are as a person. And, you can create a good impression if you choose to focus on it.

One of the primary areas of credit scoring is in the housing industry, from selling homes to renting apartments, and the use of a FICO score. FICO stands for Fair Isaac Company. This is the company that developed and keeps the top secret scoring system. FICO uses different models and adjusts the score depending on various factors such as low or high credit balances, the number of late payments, bankruptcy, or the length of time you've had certain credit cards. Fair Isaac is a third party company that provides the score to a potential lender. The lender does not calculate the score, but uses it to establish a borrower's credit worthiness. You can get more information at their Web page, http://www.fairisaac.com .

The top FICO score is 850, and a score of 700 is very good and would allow the potential borrower to qualify for A or A+ quality loans, which would have the lowest interest rates and most favorable terms. If we use mortgage rates of 4-5% as what would be the best available at the time, a person with this score would qualify for that rate. If the score was around 650, they could qualify for B- or a B+ loan and the interest rate could be 1-2% higher. With a score of 580–620, a borrower might be in the C range and find the interest rate offered is 5% higher, or maybe no loan would be offered. In addition, the loan fees are also higher.

When buying a house, besides the money a borrower would pay for obtaining a credit check, getting title insurance, paying escrow charges and appraisal fees, there is an additional cost to get most mortgage loans: *points*. Points refer to the cost of purchasing a loan. One point represents 1% of the loan balance. On a $100,000 loan this would be $1,000 to purchase the loan. If a credit score puts someone in the B or C range, the points could rise to 4, meaning $4,000 to purchase the same loan. Other fees could increase from $275 to process the same paperwork for a typical A borrower to $650 for a B or C borrower.

After all these costs and fees are paid, there is a nasty little practice many lenders have. It is primarily from lenders who have provided loans to people with less than stellar credit; they DO NOT report good payment history to any credit bureau. If they have a customer paying 10% interest on a loan for several years, with each payment made right on time, they keep this a secret. Why? Because they don't want other lenders soliciting to this customer who might refinance somewhere else because they now qualify for a 6% or 7% loan. They want to unfairly keep this customer and the extra profit they earn because the customer is paying 10%. For the lender, that 3% higher interest rate on a $100,000 mortgage loan amounts to an additional $90,000 *profit!*

In 2008 the banking industry went into a near collapse due to the practice of lending money to people when it was likely they would have difficulty repaying their loans. Property values

68

dropped below the outstanding loan amounts, payments rose and people by the thousands defaulted on their loans.

This book will support you in the process of handling money effectively and improving your credit score. You can also seek the support and assistance of Consumer Credit Counseling Service. They are a member of the National Foundation of Consumer Credit, a federally approved counseling agency, and have an office in almost every major city across the United States. Stay away from credit agencies that charge fees for their services, which often do not have your interest in mind. Why pay for services you can get for free, which may also be more reputable?

Step 4.

Acknowledge the Six Roadblocks to Financial Independence

There are six roadblocks that can slow down your progress to creating financial independence:
1. Debts
2. Economic Conditions
3. Taxes
4. Asset & Risk Management, Frauds
5. Human Problems and
6. Procrastination.

Debt can slow you down from creating financial independence. As you read in step 2, if you make minimum payments on a credit card you could pay 200–400% of retail. This applies to your home as well. A typical 30-year mortgage at 6% will have you pay back $215,838 for each $100,000 you borrow. You'll be better off both psychologically and financially the sooner you eliminate debt. But this does NOT apply to investment real estate.

Would you pay $565,904 for a new Ford? If you paid $400 per month for 48 months instead of investing that money at 12%, you would have given up over a half million dollars 30 years later for the $19,200 you made in monthly payments.

Economic conditions deal with inflation and recessions. Companies may be adding or laying off employees and these are natural cycles the economy will experience. You are in a better position to prevent this from having an impact on you by the level of training and education you have. The more knowledge you have, the better—providing you take action on what you know, and your knowledge is in a field that's growing and not shrinking. You could know everything there is to know about buggy whips, but that probably won't provide much economic security. Even if you have your own business, the concept of having more knowledge and taking action on it still applies to avoiding the impact of an economic downturn, or getting more from the economy rising.

Taxes are the fuel to support the system which gives us the opportunities and freedoms we have in the United States. There is no law, and there never has been a law, which requires anyone to pay more in income taxes than is required. The more you know about the income tax code, the more money you will save and the more money you will have available to invest for your financial freedom. Take advantage of financial planners, CPAs (Certified Public Accountants) and others who know the tax laws if you don't want to know this yourself. Be aware, you still need to know what's going on. When you sign the tax return, you are the one who is responsible, not your accountant.

As an example of advice you probably won't get from a CPA is the concept of creating wealth to avoid income taxes. Our tax structure is set up to tax income, not increases in wealth. If you own stock or real estate and it doubles in value in one year, you don't pay any income taxes on that increase in value. You do pay taxes on interest, dividends, or your personal earnings, but not on an increase in your wealth. If you sell a stock, then you have created a taxable event that would now be subject to either income or capital gains taxes. Nothing occurs unless you trigger a taxable event, like selling it.

Asset & Risk Management/Frauds are areas that represent tremendous opportunity for either growth or major setbacks. This involves insuring what you can't afford to lose, and investing in areas where you won't be ripped off. When it comes to frauds, I have file folders full of different ways people have scammed others from phony oil wells to fraudulent trust deeds and fake gold. To effectively manage and protect your assets, rely on experts you know and trust. Limit your investments to the areas you know and understand. If you don't understand it you could lose lots of money quickly and easily. I lost a huge amount of money investing in a restaurant because I was not completely and personally familiar with that business. I have made huge amounts of money in real estate because I understand it completely.

Human problems are the items such as sickness, disability, death or divorce that can cause a slow down in the creation of financial freedom. Some things can be taken care of by insurance. Others, like divorce, deal with working on relationship skills. They do not have to be messy, angry and financially devastating events. I know this from personal experience. They were costly to me, but not devastating.

Procrastination is one of the largest roadblocks to financial independence. Your first step in overcoming it is to continue to read this book. The next step is to take action on what you read. Fill out the forms, ask yourself questions, ask other people for support or referrals, pay yourself first and invest for your financial freedom. You'll learn about these items in the following section.

Where will you be at age 65?

The following are the results of not having a financial education. This is the challenge we face. This book will provide you with the tools to use so you won't have to face these dismal circumstances. This information was compiled from government data (for which your tax dollars paid) and insurance company mortality data. Mortality data is what insurance companies use to determine how long people will live, or when they'll drop dead. Insurance companies have proven to be very profitable playing the odds.

The picture looks pretty bleak at age 65. For every 100 people who start working at age 25, this is what happens 40 years later, based on figures from 2011-2014:

20% of the population won't even make it. I'm saying that almost 1 out of 5 people don't even live through the 40 years of work to retire at 65. Just think for a moment. Do you know someone who has died prior to age 65? You probably do.

10% of the remaining population, about 23 million seniors, have an income near the poverty level. In 2014 this was $11,670 per year, or $972 per month

12% will have half their income coming from Social Security which is about $1230 per month, or $14,760 per year! The poverty level for a married couple was $15,730 in 2014. The total income for people in this group is just under $30,000 per year.

16% will have a median annual income of $35,107 based on 2011 figures. The median is a half-way point. This is roughly $2925 per month. Can you picture yourself today living for the next 25 years, or longer, on $2,925 per month? And, this includes social security.

You may be reading this book well after 2014, so don't dwell on the specific income figures. Inflation will have made the income numbers higher, but the percentage of the population near the poverty level will still be around 22%. The percentage of people who will have to struggle with an inadequate income will still be around 38%. These percentages have remained virtually unchanged since 1970 when they were compiled by the Department of Health, Education and Welfare. What I've accounted for so far is 58% of the population.

Only 5%, fewer than 1 in 20, will have an income of $7000 per month, or more, after age 65, which would be considered successful. 95% of the population is either dead or dead broke by retirement age.

Do you think someone wakes up on their twenty-fifth birthday and says, "I think I'll work hard for forty years, make lots of money, spend more than I earn so I can live in poverty for the rest of my life?" No, they didn't plan to fail. What happened? They just failed to plan.

In this book, I have done everything I can to support you to take the actions necessary to create a better future for yourself. If you're willing to follow my instructions, you will have completed a five-year financial goal. It will be your goal: A goal that will be possible for you. A goal that will be your inspiration to use the tools I'll provide so you can create financial freedom.

Resources used for the statistics provided in the previous paragraphs:

http://www.aoa.gov/Aging_Statistics/Profile/2011/docs/2011profi le.pdf

http://money.cnn.com/2013/06/10/retirement/retirement-income

http://seniorjournal.com/NEWS/Politics/2009/20090225-UCLAStudySays.htm

http://www.cepr.net/index.php/blogs/beat-the-press/the-myth-of-qwealthier-seniorsq-and-cutting-social-security-and-medicare

http://www.kaiserhealthnews.org/stories/2011/november/14/afflu ent-seniors-could-take-a-hit-on-medicare.aspx

Section III

The Tools to Create Wealth

The Tools

How to Live Within Your Income in 90 Days Guaranteed (By Using the Tools!)

In the introduction, I said you would be provided with tools to make powerful new decisions. With these tools, you can make choices about who will be getting your money and determine if you're getting the level of pleasure you're paying for. Again, don't be concerned by the term "tools." Generally, tools are the forms and concepts provided which will allow you to create financial independence. If you don't like the word tools, substitute the word "keys," or anything else you're comfortable with.

If you wanted to open a locked door, you would use a key. If you wanted to prepare a gourmet meal you would need cooking tools, also called utensils, like a knife, spatula, grater, pot, pan and so on. If you wanted to repair an automobile you would need tools like a wrench, screwdriver and pliers. You wouldn't expect to build a house with your bare hands, would you? These forms and concepts are the tools that will allow you to build your financial house and attain financial freedom. This house will shelter you from fear, anxiety or concerns about your economic circumstances.

You will not need any financial background to complete these forms. I've attempted to make them as simple as possible. If you do have a financial background you will see the value in this simple approach. The wealthiest people in the world use tools similar to these. They use them to measure how they're winning in the game of life, to see if they're on track toward their goals or to determine if they're getting what they paid for. If these tools make sense for the wealthiest people in the world to use, don't you think they would be of value to you, too?

In the next several steps, you will learn about the tools to get out of debt, build an investment portfolio, and live within your income in 90 days. If you use The Financial Coach Spending Plan Register (Tool #5) as I suggest, you can live within your income in 90 days. I guarantee it!

Step 5.

How to Get Out of Debt Painlessly

You could be at one of four levels. You could be reading this book and have no issues with credit card debt. This would be level one of four levels. At the first level either you have no credit card, or if you charge something on a credit card, when the bill comes in you pay off the balance in full each month. I'm not going to be dealing with that in this program. If that's your situation, you don't have a problem with credit card debt. There may be a problem with shopping, but not debt.

At level two, you may have some debt you're carrying, and some extra money you could apply to get rid of the debt. The third level is where there is no extra money beyond the minimum payments required. The fourth level is where you don't even have the money to make the minimum payments.

I'll be explaining the best way to get rid of the debt. **Best** does **not** mean easiest or cheapest. Best means a method that is part of a new habit, attitude and skill—a skill that will prevent debt from coming back again.

LEVELS OF CREDIT CARD INDEBTEDNESS

Level one	Credit card charges paid off monthly
Level two	Carrying credit card debt with possibility of making payments above minimum.
Level three	Only able to make minimum payments on credit cards.
Level four	Unable to make minimum payments on debt.

First let's look at level three. Let's say you don't have any extra money; you can just make your minimum payments. You may want to consider a consolidation loan, or look around for a low interest credit card, or call your current creditors and ask them to reduce your interest rates.

The last suggestion I made I want you to read again. It could pay for this book 100 times over. It could save you thousands of dollars. Call your current creditors and ask them to reduce your interest rate. That's all there is to it. I had one client do this and he got a 10% interest reduction (from 23% to 13%) and he wasn't even making his payments on time. Over the course of paying off his card he saved $5,000 in interest. He did it with just one phone call. Are you willing to make a phone call if it might save you hundreds or thousands of dollars?

I suggest you don't reduce your payments just because they've reduced the interest rates. Keep the same level of payments and you'll be able to get rid of the debt sooner.

What's if you're at level four and you can't even make the minimum payments? I suggest the book by Jerrold Mundis called *How to Get Out of Debt, Stay Out of Debt, and Live Prosperously*. It is listed in the resource section, and it will tell you how to 'declare a moratorium' for a month or two so you can get your financial life in order. During this moratorium you do not pay any of your creditors. However, you do contact them to let them know you are working on your finances, intend to pay them back in full, will not be paying them for the next one or two months, and will then re-contact them with a repayment schedule, which you will do.

While it may be obvious, I'm going to warn you anyway: Regardless of whether you're at level 2, 3 or 4. DO NOT ADD ANY NEW DEBT WHILE PAYING OFF YOUR CURRENT OR OLD DEBT. If you use the tools in this book and "pay yourself first," you won't have to incur any new debt. I will go into great depth on this item later in this book.

Tool #1 - The Debt Elimination Form

This is the first tool in the Appendix and shows you *how to get out of debt, without pain.* An example of this form is shown on the next page.

Now we will discuss level two. Let's say you've got an extra $100 per month you could apply toward your credit cards, and let's say you had 10 cards. Would it make sense to send an extra $10 to each creditor? Not really. What I'm going to suggest is you take the extra $100 and you send it all to one creditor. And, the one you pick is the one that has the lowest balance, and may have the highest interest. These are usually department store cards. It's possible it may not have the highest interest. The lowest balance is the most important criteria.

On the following chart you see a $461 balance on a MasterCard at the top. I've put it at the top of the list even though the other cards have a higher interest. Again, *the lowest balance is the most important criteria.* If I add $100 to my minimum payment of $20, this balance will be wiped out in about 4 months.

Sample of the Debt Elimination Form (Tool #1 in the Appendix)

CREDITOR	BALANCE OWED	APR%	MIN. PAYMENT	PAYMENT MADE
MasterCard	$ 461	19.2	$20.00	$120
Department Store	$1,800	21.6	$80.00	
Visa	$1,800	19.8	$80.00	

Can you recall having owed money in the past and paying it off in full? How did that feel? Didn't it feel great that you did not have to pay someone anymore? Well, that's how this system works. It's about the good feelings you get paying off your debts. It's about the excitement that comes from seeing results from the actions you take.

The power of this program comes from the emotional or psychological benefits first, and the economic benefits second. You develop muscles to handle money differently. You make the decisions that, one small step at a time, will lead you to a financial independence.

Applying all the extra money to one creditor is how this tool works. You pick the one with the lowest balance but high interest, and get rid of that first. You quickly eliminated a creditor from your list. This is what I'm asking you to look for when you fill out the Debt Elimination Form in the Appendix. You then just work your way down the list.

With the first balance gone, you then add the minimum payment you just saved, plus the extra $100 to the next card on the list. In this example, it would be the Department Store; with an $80 minimum payment, you would add $100 to it. Now it's $180, plus you pick up the $20 from the MasterCard bill you don't have to pay anymore, and you'll be sending the Department Store $200 per month. In about 8 more months, instead of an additional 16 months, this debt will be paid off. Next, add $200 to the $80 Visa minimum, and pay $280 per month.

If you follow this example, you'll see all the bills get paid off in 17 months instead of 29 months—a full year of payments wiped out, and over $440 of interest saved. This is without transferring the balance to a lower rate card or even getting a rate reduction from the current creditors. This is without getting a consolidation loan.

Warning

It's time for another warning: When it comes to paying off debt the quick and easy way, it invariably returns. I've experienced this, and so has every single person I've ever met with. When someone borrows against the equity in their home, or refinances it, receives an inheritance, tax refund, wins the lottery, gets a gift from parents or others, declares bankruptcy or gets a consolidation loan to deal with what they owe, *they have learned no new skills to pay off debt and it always comes back.* Well maybe only 99% of the time; I've not met everyone in the world who has done this.

Creating financial independence, creating financial freedom comes from the skills of handling money effectively. This is what this book is about. Those quick and easy maneuvers do not produce the necessary skills. They only teach people to use a similar behavior to get themselves out of debt the next time it happens.

Step 6.

Find out where you are today

Now we're going to move from looking at credit cards or debt to the big picture, like moving our focus from one tree to a whole forest. You've been earning money doing whatever you do. You've exchanged your time and/or talents for money. Well, what do you have to show for it? Make believe you invited someone to your home. On the way they got lost and called you for directions. What would be the first question you would ask them? "Where are you?" Right? The next tool gives you the answer to the question of where you are financially.

Tool #2 - The Balance Sheet

This next tool is called a *"Balance Sheet"* and represents a major step in creating financial freedom: Finding out where you are now. The way I will explain and use this form is designed to assist you in creating financial freedom. Some of the terms I use will not fit with generally accepted accounting standards. This is done on purpose to support you by using concepts that work for ordinary people. If you are an accountant, I think you will still recognize my version of a balance sheet.

With this tool (balance sheet) you'll look at everything you own and everything you owe. It's like a snapshot of your overall financial picture and only reflects the moment in time when you fill it in. The next moment, your cash could be higher or lower. This tool will show if you are in a positive or negative financial position. You may see how some items can produce income for you when you choose to stop working for a living, and others won't. As an example, equity in a car or a home produces no income to buy groceries.

Robert Kiyosaki in his book *Rich Dad, Poor Dad* says that a home in which you live is not an asset at all, but a liability. Not only does it not create any income, it does create expenses, from the mortgage payments and property taxes to the maintenance and repairs. His book is designed to move people from what many would consider wealthy to mega wealthy. My purpose is to move people from struggle to wealth.

The value in seeing this snapshot of your balance sheet is the opportunity to create a *before and after* financial picture. First, I'll guide you in completing the form and then describe what the picture represents. Whether it's three months, six months, or one year from now, take this picture again. This is how you'll measure your progress. You'll see if you have more cash in the bank, newer cars, more investments, or less debt each time you take a new picture. The objective is to create a large, investable *Net Worth*. This is the amount you would have left over if you sold everything you owned to pay off everything you owed. *Assets* are everything you own. If you subtract what you owe from what you own it's called *Net Worth*. Liabilities are everything you owe. Even though you won't be selling everything you own, net worth is the measurement to show you how close you're getting to financial freedom.

If your eyes glazed over at this point, take a break. Call a friend and tell them what you just read. This is as close to accounting as I will get in this book. So, if you're concerned about that, you don't have to be.

First, if you own a home, estimate how much you would receive if you sold it today. This is called *Fair Market Value* (FMV). Put the total sale price without reducing it for any mortgage balance you owe. The mortgage balance amount will go under *Liabilities*. The difference between the amount you owe on the house and how much it would sell for is called *'equity.'* I'm not asking you to figure this out anywhere. I'm just defining a word I'll be using a few paragraphs from now.

If you don't have a house then this will be blank. Don't put the rent payment you make each month here; that will go on the *Cash Flow Form.*

The balance of the questions under *Assets* should be straight forward. You either have money in an Individual Retirement Account (IRA) or you don't. This would be the same for a company retirement plan like a Profit Sharing or 401(k) plan. Securities are stocks, bonds and mutual fund investments.

For life insurance cash value, this is what you would get back if you canceled the policy. This only applies to policies that build cash values such as whole life, universal life, or variable life. If it is term insurance, the cash value would be zero. Do not put how much would be paid if someone died. That would be the face amount and doesn't apply here.

If you don't know what something is, like stock options, chances are you don't have it, so don't concern yourself with it. If you're self-employed or have a business that can be sold, list the amount you would receive after paying off business debts, if it can be sold. It may have a value beyond your business equipment or inventory, or it may not. After you've listed everything you own under *Assets,* list what you owe under *Liabilities.* You would have already listed the total of your credit card debt from Tool #1 in the Appendix, so put the total where this is requested. Be sure you've included car or boat loans and debts to friends or relatives. Include back taxes and student loans, too. Write down the total amount due, not the monthly payment you make. Again, monthly payments go on the *Cash Flow Form.* (There are more suggestions following the Balance Sheet form on the next page.)

Tool #2
The BALANCE SHEET
(Another form is in the Appendix)

ASSETS

LIABILITIES
LIABILITIES

Home (FMV)* $_____

Other Real Estate   _____   Mortgage$_____

More Real Estate   _____   _____

Personal property   _____   _____

Vested retirement   _____

IRA's   _____   Credit Cards: $_____

Listed Securities   _____   _____   _____

Stock options   _____   _____   _____

Life Ins (Cash Value) _____   _____   _____

Business interest - _____   Other   Debts   (Auto, boat,

Accts receivable   _____   notes, pool loan, taxes, etc.):

Inventory/equip.   _____   _____ $_____

Cash/retain. Earn.   _____   _____   _____

Goodwill   _____   _____   _____

Personal savings -   _____   _____   _____

Money market acct.- _____   _____   _____

Certificates of   TOTAL

Deposit   _____   Liabilities: $_____

next maturity date   _____

Checking account -   _____   NET WORTH: $_____

Autos   _____   _____

             _____   _____   HOME DETAILS

Other   _____   _____   Purchase price $_____

TOTAL ASSETS $_____   Date _____

                                     Interest rate _____ %

* FMV: Fair market value.   Fixed _____ Variable _____

                                     Remaining Pmts _____

If you lease a car, it's possible the amount you owe is greater than it's value if you wanted to get out of the lease. If that's the case, put the additional amount that you would owe in the Liabilities column under Other Debts. These future payment obligations represent a liability to you for the amount above the value of the car. On the Asset side, you would not show any value for the auto, because you don't own it if you are leasing it.

Net Worth (as explained earlier) is the amount you have left over after you subtract your liabilities from your assets. This may be a positive number, and a large one, or it could be a negative number. Don't get into blame and upset if you don't like the number. It's just a number, and doesn't represent who you are as a person. This program is designed to make it a big positive number. This is the number that shows how close you are to financial independence. If you determined a $500,000 net worth would be enough so you could stop working, and your net worth was $312, it just means that you've got some work to do.

It also depends on what makes up the net worth. If it's only based on the *equity* in your home and you don't plan to sell your home, you'll need something else to provide an income. (This is where I use the word *equity* I defined in a previous paragraph.)

The other items on a *Balance Sheet* round out the picture. These are the benefits your company is providing to you if you get sick or disabled, how much life insurance your beneficiaries or family would receive if you died, and if you need to consider some estate planning like a will or living trust.

Step 7.

Getting to Where You Want to Go

Build a spending plan instead of a budget.

You need to answer the following question. And the operative word here, the key word, the important word is *like*. Do you *like* to budget? Probably not.

Let's try another question. Do you *like* to spend money? Probably. That's why I've created a spending plan instead of a budget. What I mean is you begin to spend your money in the areas that provide you the most pleasure. Well, you won't know where that is unless you find out where you've been spending your money and begin evaluating the level of pleasure you've been getting from it.

Tool #3 - The Cash Flow Form (Spending Plan)

In the next chart, you'll see a sample of the *Cash Flow Form*. The Appendix has the complete form. You will use this tool to find out where all the money you earn or receive comes from and where you're spending it. It's also referred to as an Income and Expense form and creates the basis of the "spending plan." After you fill out this form you need to ask yourself, "Is this is how I want to spend my money?"

Income

___

You may receive a regular paycheck as your only source of income, so the income side will be easy to complete. My suggestion is to write down the amount of your net check. This is the amount after taxes have been removed and other deductions have been taken. This is the amount to look at. This is the amount you have to live on. This is the amount you have available to pay your bills. Looking at the gross amount will not serve you unless it stimulates you to take actions to reduce your taxes and other deductions and transfer that money into the areas that will create wealth.

You may be a commission sales person. If that's the case you have a different source of income. You may be an entrepreneur, a businessperson, or self-employed. You may find you have several sources of income. You may have income from rental property, dividends, interest or royalties. You may be retired and have income from social security, a military pension or a corporate retirement plan. You may be someone who doesn't have to work because you get distributions from a trust account or you can't work and receive disability income. Just fill out the *Cash Flow Form* based on where the money comes from now. If this income will stop, be sure to make a note of it.

The CASH FLOW FORM (Sample - Complete form is in the Appendix)

INCOME
Client $_____
Significant Other _____

EXPENSE
Person # __
1. House pmt./rent$_____
(Other house exp.,
maid, gardener _____

Category #s appear out of sequence, but relate to Tool #4, see it for numerical listings & details.

Bonus	$_____	18. Property taxes $_____ *
Commission	_____	13. Other Real Estate loans _____
Rents	_____	18. Other RE taxes _____ *
Interest	_____	Other RE expense _____
Dividends	_____	2. Auto: loans/lease _____
Notes received	_____	parking/gas _____
Royalties	_____	maintenance/repairs _____ *
Side business	_____	registration fees _____ *
Trust distribution	_____	3. Food: groceries _____
Social Security	_____	meals out _____
Retirement plan	_____	4. Clothing _____ *
Other	_____	5. Personal care _____
		6. Health care _____
The above figures are:		7. Entertainment _____
Monthly	__	8. Gifts _____ *
Annual	__	9. Education _____
Pay periods are:		10. Vacations _____ *
1 time a month	__	11. Business Expense _____
2 times a month	__	12. Dependent care _____
every 2 weeks	__	13. Regular Save/Invest _____

*The category items on the Cash Flow Form, like clothing, gifts, and vacations, are items which may not show up each month, but you need to set money aside monthly for those items.

You'll notice at the top of the column over the expenses it says *person #____*. If you're part of a couple, or even a group of people who live together and contribute income to the same household, you'll need to copy this form for each person. Or, you can add a column next to the one on the form if there are just two people. As an alternative look at the form (Tool #3A) that follows the Cash Flow Form in the Appendix. Any couple can use this tool to determine how to share expenses, whether they live together or not.

If you get paid once or twice a month, this is pretty easy. However, if you get paid every two weeks, then this form works a little differently for you. There will be two months each year when you will receive an extra, or third paycheck. I do ***not*** want this extra paycheck to be considered or added into your monthly income. It would slightly increase what your monthly income would look like, and this would be misleading, because it would not be a true reflection of what actually comes in ten months of the year. You can certainly look at this as additional income, but it would be more valuable for you to save it, rather than needing it to bail you out of the short-falls you've had 10 months of the year.

If you're self-employed or have your own business with an erratic income this exercise is more important for you. For this part, take the total you earned for a 12-month period, and average it out on this form under gross income. It may not be accurate, but it's an important starting point. You may be short one month, and play catch up in another. The goal setting part of this book is designed to assist you to establish an action and support structure; you get to focus on what needs to be done to create a consistent and/or higher income and deal with the peaks and valleys in your income. I've done it, and I know you can do it, too.

Referring back again to Robert Kiyosaki's book, *Rich Dad, Poor Dad*, how your cash flows from one area to another on your balance sheet will determine if you will be poor, middle-class, or wealthy. The poor use their income to directly pay for expenses such as food, rent, clothes, fun, transportation, and so on. People in the middle-class use their income for those same expenses plus liabilities such as a mortgage, consumer loans, or credit cards. The wealthy use their income to purchase assets that generate income, such as rental property, stocks, bonds, intellectual property, trust deeds or notes. And, the wealthy have their income come from things like rent, royalties, interest, and dividends. Completing this form will allow you to see where you are now. Then you can choose where you want to go.

Expenses

From a *Dear Abby* column:
"I am a twenty-three-year-old liberated woman who has been on the pill for two years. It's getting expensive and I think my boyfriend should share half the cost, but I don't know him well enough to discuss money with him."

The above comments say it better than I can. People are more willing to discuss sex than money. In the privacy of your own home you've written down where your money comes from. Now, let's see where it's going.

Again, the *Cash Flow Form*, where you list both your income and expenses, is in the Appendix in the back of the book. When you fill it out for the first time it's okay to guess. It's even desirable if you don't have the information available. You'll need to photocopy it before you begin to fill it out so you will have extra copies for future use. **Tool #4** in the Appendix is the Spending Plan *Cash Flow Memory Jogger*. You may want to look over the items in each category to remind you of the places where you could have spent money but forgot about it. A sample, and more of an explanation of the Cash Flow Memory Jogger, follows in a few pages. Again, the complete list is in the Appendix.

Another way to fill out the *Cash Flow Form* is to wait a month or two so you can track your money to find out where it's going. I do *not* suggest this. Instead, I suggest you **guess first**, and then you can track your expenses and compare that to your guesswork. Again, this is why you need to copy the form before you fill it out the first time. You'll be coming back to this form several times.

In addition, this form needs to be used by each person in the household who is responsible for some expenses. When I refer to financially responsible, it usually excludes children. If you and another person decide to share expenses, like you pay the rent and the other person pays the utilities, each of you needs to fill out a form. If you give a child an allowance, that just goes down under dependent expense for you. Likewise, if your significant other has no responsibility for expenses, but you give them money, it could be treated like giving an allowance to a child. If it's a roommate arrangement, they don't have to complete a form. You just omit from your form the expenses they pay for.

I've had clients whose husbands made none of the financial decisions or paid any of the bills. They may or may not have worked and earned an income. They might have just turned their paycheck over to their wife and received an allowance in return. In this situation, there would be no need for the husband to fill out a form. The wife would just put the allowance down under dependent expense. The same would hold true if the roles are reversed.

After you fill out the *Cash Flow Form* for the first time by guessing wherever the money went, or looking back through your checkbook register and compiling it from your credit card statements, subtract the expense figure from the income figure to see if you have a deficit (spending more than you earn) or if you have a surplus. If the amount on this line is positive, great! You now know how much money you have to use to either reduce debt or increase your savings and investments. Setting aside this surplus is one way to create financial freedom, but this is *paying yourself last*. The ability to have work as a choice and not as a requirement comes from having money that generates the income for you to live on. Otherwise, you have to continue to generate the income. This is called money at work instead of you at work. In Step 10 I'll tell you the most powerful way of building this pool of money. It's called pay yourself first.

If the amount on your cash flow form is negative, guess what? You're spending more than you earn. I apologize if this is too basic. I used to think all I had to do when I saw this in my situation was to earn more money. After my expenses outran my six-figure income, I realized it wouldn't matter how much I earned, I had to start dealing with the expenses. While some people may joke that this is the "American way," it will lead you to personal financial ruin. I know that is not the course you want to take or you would not be reading this book.

There are two solutions to a deficit. After you complete the *Cash Flow Form*, you'll be ready to deal with the first solution to overspending: *The Financial Coach Spending Plan Register*. We will get to that in a few pages. The other solution will be shown in Step 9: "What to do when expenses exceed income."

If two people work together I suggest they determine what expenses they will be responsible for ahead of time in writing, as they complete the *Cash Flow Form*. Use **Tool #3a** in the Appendix to assist with this process. It can be changed whenever you like, but start by writing it down. Then each person has their own checking account to cover their own expenses. I didn't say checkbook, I said checking account. The income is split along the lines of who will pay for expenses. It doesn't matter who earned more or how much, the money gets split by the expenses each person agreed to be responsible for paying. This includes vacations, hobbies or whatever. An excellent book to assist with the mechanics of this budget/spending plan process is *Rich on Any Income* by Combs and Christensen. It was first published about 25 years ago, but is still on Amazon. An excellent book for couples who have difficulty communicating in this area is *Couples and Money* by Victoria F. Collins. It was originally published by Bantam Books but is now available through Gabriel Publications, online at Amazon.com. This is the best book in the field and bringing it back to the public was the reason I established my publishing company.

Tool #4 - The Spending Plan, Cash Flow Memory Jogger

The fourth tool in the Appendix is the *Cash Flow Memory Jogger*. Take a look at the sample that follows. You can tear out the page in the Appendix or copy it to carry with you. It will remind you of the different expenses and categories. The first place you'll use it is when you sit down to fill in the *Cash Flow Form* and can't remember all the places where you spent your money. It will remind you, and it matches the numbers on the expense list. As an example, someone might say, "I don't buy clothes or spend money on entertainment. I don't have any expenses there." But they do if they go to the dry cleaners or laundry. Those are clothing expenses. They do if they buy books, magazines, CDs, rent videos or pay for Cable TV. Those are entertainment expenses. There should be no "miscellaneous" items. If it's not on the list, and it's legal, call me and let me know what it is, and I'll add it to the next edition. There are 20 different categories I've created to find out where your money is going and I believe this would cover almost any place you could be spending it. You can also use these categories in a computer spreadsheet program or with existing programs like *Quick Books or Microsoft Money*.

There's an unusual category on the *Spending Plan Cash Flow Memory Jogger*. It's item #19, called *Lessons Learned*. This covers situations when you've spent money and you don't really have anything to show for it, other than the fact you've learned a lesson. This could be anything from being ripped off in an investment scam to buying a vacation timeshare you never use, and find out you paid twice what it was worth. This isn't an investment, or capital loss, it's a lesson learned.

Sample of listings from the Cash Flow Memory Jogger:

1. Home/Shelter
   A. Mortgage or Rent
   B. Miscellaneous:
      1. Maintenance
      2. Gardener, Maid...
      3. Purchases
      4. Home Assoc. Dues
      5. Alarm service
2. Auto/Transportation
   A. Car payment/lease
   B. Gasoline/fuel
   C. Parking
   D. Registration
   E. Oil/lube
   F. Maintenance
   G. Repair
   H. Accessories
   I. Bus/Taxi
   J. Air Fare
   K. Other/
3. Food
   A. Groceries
   B. Meals Out
   C. Snacks

4. Clothing
   A. Apparel, Vacation
   B. Shoes
   C. Accessories
   D. Jewelry
   E. Tailor
   F. Cleaners
   G. Laundry
   H. Shoe Repair
5. Personal Care
   A. Toiletries
   B. Cosmetics
   C. Manicure
   D. Pedicures
   E. Haircuts
   F. Massage
   G. Spa/Gym
6. Health Care
   A. Doctor
   B. Dentist

These forms were developed over many years of trial and error with thousands of people. If you feel these forms, or this book, would be of value to another person, loan them a copy, or suggest they buy a copy, or they can get a copy at the library and have all of the information. Just having the forms alone may not be enough.

Step 8.

How to Use the Most Powerful Tool to Track Expenses and Measure Your Pleasure

The following tool will let you know in *5 to 10 seconds* how much money you will have available to spend in any category you choose to track, without using a computer! In addition, you have the opportunity to measure your pleasure: You will be able to see if you're receiving the level of pleasure you are paying for based on the questions you can ask as you make a purchase.

Tool #5: The Financial Coach Spending Plan Register

You've now guessed at your expenses and determined if you have a positive or negative cash flow from the Income and Expense form. Now it's time to verify the figures. In the back of the book, I provide you with two pages of *The Financial Coach Spending Plan Checkbook Register* you can tear out and copy. There are two ways to use this form in the following example.

103

Also, refer back to the *Spending Plan Cash Flow Memory Jogger* for assistance in setting up categories for yourself.

When you fill out *The Financial Coach Spending Plan Checkbook Register* for the first time, use it find out where your money is going. Simply pick from any of the categories on the *Cash Flow Memory Jogger* for the category where money leaks out during the month. It may be meals out, groceries, clothing, transportation expenses or entertainment.

You don't need to use the register to write down your rent or mortgage payment. After all, once you've paid this, it doesn't show up again for another month. I do not suggest bi-weekly mortgage payments. There are ways to reduce your mortgage that provide better recordkeeping than this method. Also, it appears one of the country's most popular companies that performed this service committed fraud and embezzlement. In October of 1994, Bi-Weekly Mortgage Acceptance Corporation, better known as Billie Mac, collapsed. It was shut down by court order. Its president, Jeffrey R. Brown, was charged with the theft of more than $1.3 million worth of homeowner funds.

In the following example, I use the categories *Meals Out* and Groceries to illustrate the primary two ways the register is used. A third use is to show how well you're saving up for something. When saving up for something, like a $3,000 vacation, put the goal at the top. As you set aside money toward this, subtract from the goal to see how much you have left to save.

In the example you'll notice for Meals Out, on January 1, I spent $10 for lunch. It was cash. I have the room for notes to show who I had lunch with, and this is also valuable at tax time. When I'm having business meals it can be noted here. (In my register, I actually keep two separate columns, one for personal meals and one for business meals. You can structure your own register to gather any data you want).

It's so simple to keep the records because it's right with my checkbook that I always carry. A client of mine wraps his cash in the register like a money clip. He uses more cash, and I use more checks.

I don't have to wait until I get home and load it in some computerized money tracking, budgeting or check writing program to have some answers. I don't have to fumble around in a three-ring binder, iPhone, Blackberry, or Franklin Planner. It's right where the money came from. If you choose to use a program on a "smart phone" that's fine. Just make a notation with every single expenditure right then and there.

So, if I spent $10 having lunch with Bill I write it in the column. Let's say the next day I use a credit card at lunch and charge $22 on Visa. I put a circle around the $22 because this identifies money I spent I didn't have. At any time I can go through my register and, by adding up all of the circled items, I know how much will show up on my credit card statement when it arrives in the mail.

For the Smith business lunch, I add the $22 to the $10 I spent previously and it tells me so far I've spent $32 in *Meals Out*. The shaded area is for additional notes and the subtotal. The next day I go out to dinner and charge $26 on my American Express. Again, I circle the number. Now I see I've spent a total of $56 in *Meals Out*. On the fourth, I write check #123 for a dinner with my wife. I spent $22. You can see I've spent a total of $80 in *Meals Out*. It's just that simple. I write it down and add it up. It takes no more than 5–10 seconds after each expenditure.

Category: Meals Out			
		Plan to spend: $_____	
cash		Last Month Balance: $ *None*	
credit		New amount to spend: $_____	
check	Date	Notes	Amount
cash	1/1	Lunch with Bill	$10.00
visa	1/2/98	Smith Business Lunch	(22)
		Subtotal	32
amex	1/3	Dinner W/wife	(26)
			58
#123	1/4	Dinner W/wife	22
			80
		Measure your pleasure	(+) (OK) or (-)

Category: Groceries			
		Plan to spend: $ 300	
cash		Last Month Balance: $ <25>	
credit		New amount to spend: $ 275	
check	Date	Notes	Amount
cash	1/3	Vons	25.00
		subtotal	250.00
#124	1/5	Safeway	31.00
			219.00

Measure Your Pleasure

In the book *Your Money or Your Life*, two key concepts are presented. In the first, money is converted to life energy you've used up. Any income level can be converted into an hourly rate. That hourly rate is used to measure the cost of items you purchase. As an example, a common work week of 40 hours would be 2000 hours per year. If your annual income were $30,000, you would reduce it by the taxes you pay and the other deductions from your check. You would then add up the additional hours you spend related to your work, such as driving there, bringing work home, buying or cleaning work clothes, and so on and add that to get to the real total of hours you spend related to your work. In this example, it would reduce the hourly rate from $15 ($30,000 ÷ 2000 hours per year) to $10.67. ($24,000 after taxes divided by 2,250 hours.) You are trading each hour of your life energy for $10.67.

The next step is to use the concept of asking questions. You use the hourly rate of life energy given up to measure the level of pleasure you get for the money you spent. As an example, repairing your car for $426 isn't spending $426. It's giving up 40 hours of your life to repair the car. Now, you ask questions like, "Did I receive pleasure and value based on how much I spent?" "Is this expense in alignment with my values?" "Would I spend money in this way if I didn't have to work for a living?" I also suggest you do this for items you don't track, like rent, mortgage or car payments. Based on your answers, you put a rating at the bottom of the various expense category columns.

If your answer is positively strong put a plus (+) sign at the bottom of the spending plan column or next to the payment in your checkbook. If it was fine at its current level, put "O.K." If it was unsatisfactory, or you would like to see it decrease, put a minus sign (-). You can measure a whole category, or item by item; it's your choice.

Now that you've discovered where you're spending your money by writing it down in *The Financial Coach Spending Plan Register*, you're ready for the second and primary way it's used. This is shown in the *Groceries column*. Here I decided I only need, or choose, to spend $300 on groceries. I arrived at this figure based on finding out what I usually spend on groceries and the level of pleasure that amount of money provides to me. I used the system described in the previous paragraph.

You'll notice where it shows *last month's balance* there's a negative $25. This means in the previous month instead of spending $300, I spent $325. What I do is subtract $25 from the $300 I planned to spend. I am only going to spend $275 this month. *I guarantee you can live within your income in 90 days if you use this tool as described.*

There is another way I could handle the $25 shortage. If there was money left over in another category, like Entertainment, I could reduce the amount I plan to spend there and transfer some of that money to the Groceries column, or vice versa.

On January 2, I spent $25 at Vons. I subtract that from my $275 and have $250 left. The next day I write a check to Safeway for $31. I now have $219 left. By doing this, *instantly*, I know how much money I have left to spend on groceries, or *any category* I choose to track.

Let's say it's halfway through the month, I buy some groceries and I have $100 left. Right then and there, immediately, I know I've got to slow down. I've got one-third of the money left and half the month to go. This tool yields instant information on where your money is going and how much you have left to spend in any category you choose to track. In the Appendix you'll find a sample *Spending Plan Register* which you can tear out and use.

One day I watched a television program on the life of John D. Rockefeller. This is the man who established the Standard Oil Company and at one time was the richest man in the world. The TV program showed a ledger (or register) he used when he was eleven years of age. In it, he tracked every penny that came into and out of his life, where it came from and where he spent it. These are the habits of the wealthiest people in the world and you can use them to transform your life. It's not about penny pinching. It's about consciously choosing where you will spend your money, measuring the level of pleasure it provides, and spending in alignment with the results you want to produce in your life. Your spending will be based on your values, not the values of your neighbors, co-workers or politicians. If these habits benefited the wealthiest people in the world, don't you think they would also benefit you?

Here are some valuable, helpful and powerful guidelines when it comes to spending or borrowing money:

When you excited about buying something, like a new car, new clothes, whatever, DO NOT MAKE A DECISION THAT DAY. Wait two to three days for small purchases. Wait one to two weeks before making a decision on a large purchase.

When you are stressed, or in fear, you cannot make a good selling decision, like you're behind on a mortgage, rent payment, car payment, a stock has declined due to a market crash, etcetera. In those situations do not sell an asset when influenced by fear, scarcity or lack. Next, before selling, speak to an expert, like your CPA, an attorney, or "neutral" investment advisor. It's best to get input from at least two experts and three would be preferred. This will also take the time that will allow you to cool down.

Finally, do not borrow money when you are excited or afraid.

Step 9.

What To Do When Expenses Exceed Income

When income and expenses don't balance, you have to look at three areas: *Discretionary, Variable, and Fixed* expenditures.

Discretionary expenses are the ones you have complete control over. It may be going to the movies, meals out, personal trainer, vacations, or clothing. Anything where you have complete choice is a discretionary expense.

The next expenses to look at are those that are *Variable*. These are the expenses that show up month-in and month-out. The only difference is the amount of the expense. As an example, you'll have a food bill every month. It could be higher or lower from one month to the next based on what you buy. Your utility bills, such as telephone, gas and electric, will come in month after month, but they may be higher or lower depending on usage or time of year.

You may be saying to yourself, "I know this stuff." My response is: *don't make statements* when you hear something you may know. This closes your mind to possibilities and ideas that can create the change you're looking for. When you hear something you already know, *ask questions instead*. What do you think would be more powerful? "I can't use that information in my situation" or "*How* can I use that information in my situation?" and "*What* could I do that I haven't done yet?"

You'll notice I emphasized the words *how* and *what*. Most successful people recognize they create powerful changes and transformations in their lives based on the questions they ask versus the statements they make. You'll notice these are *how* questions. Many people ask themselves *why questions*, like "Why do I get customers or clients who are jerks?" Or, "Why do I have co-workers who are rude?" *Why* questions are **not** quality questions. They create endless loop answers that do not lead to solutions. If you found out why you had customers who are jerks or co-workers who are rude, all you would have is the answer as to why. You would still have rude customers or co-workers. If what you want is nice customers or co-workers, you could ask a how or what question. *How* questions produce value through the answers you create. *How* questions are powerful. They can create the changes in your life that produce profits, fun, and anything else you choose. You could ask, "How can I get nice customers?" Or, "What do I need to do to have co-workers speak respectfully to me?" How and what questions lead to solutions. Why questions lead to generally useless answers.

The last expense area to look at is the *fixed* expenses. These are the ones that come in every month and don't change. It's your rent or mortgage payment, car payment, insurance payments. It could be the minimum payment on credit cards, and even these can be changed as well.

As an example regarding rent, I had someone working for me who was struggling to pay $625 per month on a one-bedroom apartment. (In Los Angeles, this was obviously many years ago.) I suggested she go out and get a two-bedroom apartment for $800/mo. She questioned, "Rennie, how could you possibly suggest that when I can't afford the $625 now?" Simple, if she got a roommate to share her $800 rent, she would reduce her cost to $400 per month, saving $225 per month.

I had another client who owned a boat free and clear which was docked at the marina. He was still spending $250 per month to store it. He hardly used it the year before, but still had to pay to have it painted and re-canvassed. I asked him how much it would cost to rent a boat like that, and he responded, "Oh, at least $100 a day." And he was spending $240 per month just to keep it parked at the marina. He decided to sell the boat, and when he wanted to go out he could rent something twice as nice. He eliminated a fixed monthly cost and now doesn't have to spend any money on upkeep either. What do you have in your life that's like this?

With regard to credit card minimum payments, you may recall I discussed the book, *How to Get Out of Debt* by Jerrold Mundis. You can create a credit moratorium and a repayment schedule that shows how to make payments less than the minimum. You can also get more information on this by contacting the organizations mentioned in the next paragraph.

If re-organizing or consolidating your debts, if selling assets isn't enough so that the figures balance, it may be time for you to consult one-on-one with a financial planner who specializes in this area. Or, consult with some credit assistance organization like Consumer Credit Counseling Service or Debtors Anonymous (DA.) DA is a 12-step program along the lines of the support group Alcoholics Anonymous. It's designed to help people stay away from unsecured debt and deal with money and spending issues. Information on how to reach these groups, and more, can be found on the Internet.

All of these programs are vehicles that can help you create financial freedom if you utilize them. Just like I emphasized regarding achieving your goals, *you do not have to do this by yourself.* Involve your spouse, if you have one. Involve a friend, go to some organization, become a member of a support group. *You don't have to do this by yourself.* Don't let feelings of shame stop you from opening yourself up to assistance and support. Most of the population feels they're supposed to know this stuff, and they don't. They are just as afraid as you might be to let anyone else find out they don't know these things either. As soon as you ask for support, other people will feel free to shed light on what they need to know. Don't let shame be your trap. The people who are transforming their relationship with money are not doing it through books alone. They are not doing it by themselves. They are getting together with like-minded people and getting support for the changes they want to make in their lives. You can use this book as a guide to create a group of friends or co-workers who are willing to support one another.

Step 10.

Creating Financial Freedom

In previous sections I've frequently described that financial freedom is having work as a choice instead of a requirement, or money at work so you don't have to work. This is the point in time where you don't have to depend on anyone else for your income, and I expect you to be free from consumer debt. You'll be independent of a job, career, and even free of government support. You will have a level of income from your investments that will cover your standard of living. It could be as simple as food, utilities, minimum taxes, entertainment, travel, and contributions to the communities or organizations of your choice. There are two ways of creating financial freedom, and they both start with saving some money.

The first way could be to pay all your expenses first, and then if there's some money left over you save it. This is not a trick question: What might be some good reasons for saving money? Obviously since we've been talking about financial independence this could be one reason. But what else? You could save for the down payment on a home, or second home, or income property, a vacation, new car, more education for yourself or for children's education, emergencies, opportunities, or starting a new business. There are lots of good reasons for saving money, and this first method is one way to do it. When there is money left over at the end of the month, if there is, you set it aside in savings. *See circle number 1.*

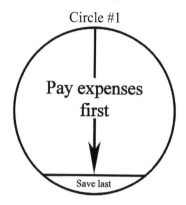

Circle #1

Pay expenses first

Save last

The preferred method would be to save first, as in *circle number 2.* Save a bigger percentage of your income before you pay your expenses. Set aside 10, 15 or maybe 20% of your income. This is what I did. This is what Jerry Buss did. Remember Jerry Buss? He's the person who purchased the Los Angeles Forum, the Lakers basketball team, Kings hockey team and the estate of Douglas Fairbanks, Jr. and Mary Pickford.

Right about here I usually get the question, "Should I be saving 10% of my income now, when I have all this debt I need to pay off?" My answer is yes and no. What I'm suggesting is *you still must pay yourself first*. It may not be 10%. Maybe it'll be 4%, or $10 per week. But pay yourself something first. This will become very clear later on when I discuss the very high cost of waiting to invest.

This is where I ask another question: *"Do you deserve to own some of the money you're earning?"* If you do, prove it! Pay yourself first. Pay yourself before you pay the telephone bill, the groceries, rent or transportation expenses. If you want to feel like you deserve to own some of the money you earn, you have to treat yourself like you do. And that means

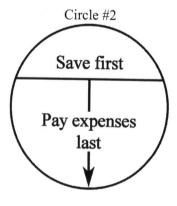

Circle #2

Save first

Pay expenses last

pay yourself first. You can't wait until you feel like it first. When the action comes first, it will create the feeling.

116

After you've paid yourself first, then pay your expenses. And a part of the expenses will be your credit card or other debts. When they're paid off, then you can dramatically increase the percentage you pay yourself first.

Paying yourself first is not a new concept. The Richest Man in Babylon is a book written in 1936 based on some clay tablets found around the turn of the century. The tablets were between 3,000 and 5,000 years old from the city of Babylon, when it was one of the wealthiest city-states on earth. The tablets tell the story of a man who got into financial trouble in Babylon, fled the city, and decided to return and clean up his act. Across 5,000 years of time, the reader is exposed to how people were taught to handle money, the excuses they had, and what it took to create wealth. As you read history, you discover people have not changed materially in 5,000 years. And, the principles of creating wealth are the same today as they were 5,000 years ago. *Pay yourself first.*

Maybe you're saying, "I can't pay myself first and have the money I need to support my standard of living." Here's what I've seen: Someone pays all their bills one month, and among them is a phone bill for $100. At the end of the month there's nothing left.

The next month they pay all their bills and among them is a phone bill for $150. Somehow they manage to pay the phone company an extra $50. I'll venture to say that different things come up each month, and someone else gets more money from you than they did in a previous month, and you still end up with nothing at the end of the month. What's missing here is putting yourself at the top of the list before the bills are paid. You'll find some way to have nothing at the end of the month, but this time you will have some money for yourself. Again, this is how financial freedom is created.

One of my clients, an attorney, said he couldn't possibly pay himself first. He told me he had $6,000 of bills to pay and had only received $5,500. He said, "How can I pay myself first when I'm short $500 to pay the bills?" (I find many people can relate to this, as it may have happened to them, or even be happening now.) I suggested he set aside $250, or about 5%, of what came in. I showed him he now had only $5,250 to pay towards $6,000 of bills. He was now short $750 instead of $500, and I asked, "What difference does it make? You're short either way." But now, he has $250 that belongs to him. He can look at that money and say he has something for the work he did. He's not just a conduit for money to flow in one end and out the other, with *nothing* to show for it. Now he has something to show for it, even if it's only $250. And psychologically, that $250 can spur him on to generate more income because now he sees he can have some of it for himself, instead of just paying bills with it.

One client, a business owner, said he did not deserve to own any of the money he was earning. He was in serious debt and even had a savings account seized for payroll taxes he owed. He said he owed too much money to others and therefore didn't deserve to own any of the money he earned. It was that attitude which prevented him from generating more income to deal with his creditors and support his family. Again, there is a psychological shift that occurs when you treat yourself like you deserve to own some of the money you earn. It allows you to generate more money. You no longer see yourself as a pipe, with money flowing in one end and out the other. The feeling that 'no matter how much comes in, you still won't have anything' will be eliminated when you pay yourself first.

This is another example of how you can justify paying yourself first. Around 1982, Western Airlines announced to its flight attendants that it was in a financial crisis. They asked the attendants to vote on taking a 23% pay cut, or laying off 23% of them.

The attendants voted to have a job with a 23% pay cut rather than face the possibility of no job at all. I've met some of them. They still had a place to live, a car to drive, food to eat and so on. They lost 23% of their income up front, money they could have used to pay themselves first. When it was taken away, they figured out how to live on less.

In your situation, it will not be taken away. It will be yours to keep for the rest of your life. It becomes the money that will create the income so you no longer have to work, unless you choose to.

How smart do you have to be to do this? If someone has an IQ of 70–80 they're smart enough. One of the people in my workshop told me about her retarded cousin. (Forget the politically correct terms. This is what the cousin said; his IQ was tested at 90.) He was told when he was young he *had to* (read no choice) put 25% of his paycheck into savings. Because of his low IQ he was only able to get minimum wage jobs. At the time the story was told to me in 1990, he was in his mid-30s and had accumulated over $90,000 in savings. Maybe you're too smart and that's why it won't work. You can figure out clever reasons why you don't have to do this. Sometimes we're too smart for our own good. Her cousin was too stupid to do anything other than what he was told. Maybe stupidity helps.

Do you recall the figures I gave you early in the book that only 16% of our population has twice the income of the poverty level at their retirement age? And do you recall that only about 5% are financially independent. The others need government assistance to maintain their lifestyle. Well, in the city of Babylon 5,000 years ago, only 10% of the population had the discipline to pay themselves first and they created one of the wealthiest city-states in the ancient world. The United States is one of the wealthiest countries in the world today, and we have 10% of our population with the discipline to pay themselves first. Not much has changed in 5,000 years. For you to think you'll be an exception to history is to court disaster. How about using what's proven effective for 5,000 years?

Step 11.

How to Handle Emergency Spending (Without Creating a Financial Disaster)

Now, where do you put the money when you paid yourself first? I have two approaches. A simple savings allocation shown in the following circle, and a more sophisticated approach I will illustrate later. You can set aside 40–60% of the money you pay yourself first into long-term savings or investments. I'll provide suggestions on where to put it in Step 12. This allocation I'm referring to often creates confusion, so I'm going to provide shocking simplicity.

In order to create financial freedom, and pay off past debts, and be prepared for future expenses, you must not only spend less than you earn today, you must set a portion aside for tomorrow. Working with thousands of people I've discovered the following: About 10–20% of what people earn needs to be set aside today to be spent later. When you add up non-monthly expenses like car repairs, registration, vacations, gifts, clothing and so on, the average is 10% of current earnings. If this is not set aside, then it won't be available later, and this is how credit card debts are built up and kept.

In addition, 10% needs to be set aside for your financial independence. This means, on average, 20-25% of what you earn today must be set aside for the future. 10-15% will be spent later, and 10% will be kept for the rest of your life.

The following circle represents a simplified allocation of the 25% that needs to be set aside each time you receive money. It shows 50% to long-term savings and investments and 50% to spend later. I've found this to be a typical allocation based on the 10% and 15% from the previous paragraph. If all you can start with is to set aside 10% of your income, then 5% would go to long-term and 5% would go to spend later. While yours could be slightly different, like 40/60, I want to keep it simple, *and any allocation is better than none at all*. More on this topic next.

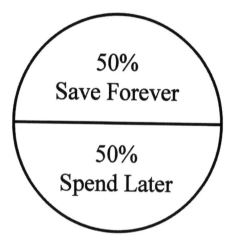

A. Simple savings allocation

When you go to the bank and ask what types of accounts they have, they'll generally tell you they have two primary types of accounts: checking and *saving*. For most people this is not true.

For most people the banks have checking and spending accounts. Most people who open up savings accounts only save up money until they have enough to buy something. I don't consider that a savings account, I say that's a spending account.

I'll explain shortly that you will open an account like this, but it won't be for long-term savings.

When I say savings, I mean *save for the rest of your life*, not save for a new car or vacation. I mean to save to create financial freedom. The money for a vacation or car goes into a spending account, which the *bank* calls a savings account.

What are some of the ways you could be paying yourself first and putting it away for long-term use? You could put it into a mutual fund by dollar-cost-averaging, a life insurance policy (whole life, universal or variable life), payroll deduction into a credit union or 401(k) plan, or automatic withdrawals for the down payment on your first or second piece of real estate. 50% of the money you pay yourself first will never leave your hands again, unless it's going into an investment that will be part of creating your financial freedom. Again, I'll go into more detail in Step 12.

50% of the money goes into what the bank calls a savings account. You know this is a spending account. Half of this money can be for an opportunity or emergency and the other half can be for emotional spending. This is where the money comes from which gets spent on things you're rarely prepared for, like the car breaking down, or the water heater which needs to be replaced, or the semi-annual insurance premium or property tax bill, or the unexpected medical expense.

Half of the money in this planned spending account is for emotional purchases. With half of the money here you can now buy something and not feel guilty about it because you hadn't planned on making the purchase. It could be for a weekend trip you need, just to get away. It could be to purchase a gift for someone, or even yourself. The money was there waiting, you just didn't know what it was for when you put it away. Take out the money and buy what you want, and don't feel guilty. Isn't that a great way to buy something? This is the practice which will allow you to get away from using credit cards in an emergency. You now have cash to use.

Again, the 50/50 or 40/60 split is a useful rule of thumb for the amount to go into the future spending account. On the *Cash*

Flow Form you'll notice small stars (*) next to some items such as auto repairs, auto registration, clothing, vacations and others. This represents items most people don't spend money on each month, but will spend money on during the course of a year. As an example, you might not be purchasing clothing each month, but you might go out and only purchase clothing twice per year. If you spend $600 each time you go, that would $1,200 for the year. If you divide that by 12 months, then it would be the same as if you spent $100 per month. This $100 per month needs to be accounted for or set aside somehow. This is what the planned spending account is for. If you add up all of the starred items from the *Cash Flow Form* it will generally be about 10% of your take-home pay. As discussed earlier, that's the rule of thumb. For the expenses that come up sporadically during the year, you need to set aside about 10% of your take-home pay each month to be prepared for them. Check for your situation, it might be 15%, or it may need to be 20%. Otherwise, when these expenses show up, you have no money to draw from, and you have to use a credit card. Again, this is the practice that will allow you to get away from using credit cards in an emergency because you will have cash to use.

B. A more sophisticated plan for periodic or sporadic expenses.

If you want to get more sophisticated, look at the next example. It shows how to plan for annual, semi-annual, periodic or even sporadic expenses. This is for the "spend later" amount that you know you'll spend for expenses that don't show up monthly. The strategy is to cover the expenses you know you'll have during the year, but you may not know when some of them may happen, like when the car will break down.

Start by looking over all of the starred expense categories for items that *do not* occur each month, but can be broken down into a monthly amount such as property taxes, annual insurance premiums, auto maintenance, vacation, a major purchase, or school tuition. Now divide the annual amount by 12.

Example:

Property taxes, annual	$1200 ÷ 12	=	$100.00
Life Insurance, semi-annual	1800 ÷ 6	=	300.00
Auto Maintenance, last year	1020 ÷ 12	=	85.00
Vacation, last year	3000 ÷ 12	=	250.00
Next car down pmt. 2 yrs.	5000 ÷ 24	=	208.33
Tuition, due in 7 months	1995 ÷ 7	=	100.00
TOTAL TO SAVE EACH MONTH		=	$1228.33

Each month, you will write a check for $1228.33 and deposit it in the planned spending account. When the insurance bill comes two months after you start this program, there will be over $2,400 available to pay the premium. When each expense comes due, all of the money will be available because it is very unlikely everything will come due all at once. When you're ready to buy the new car, you will have saved up the down payment. Whether or not you can sell the old car won't matter.

There are other expenses you know will show up: A life insurance bill you know will arrive in July; property taxes in December or April; tuition bills and things of that nature. What I'm suggesting is you divide the expense by the number of months before it comes due, and set aside that amount of money each month.

Whether you elect to use the simple approach or the sophisticated approach, *this is a crucial exercise*. With the Cash Flow Form (Tool #3) and using Step 11, you can calculate if you're actually bringing in the level of income you need for all of the expenses you have, not just the ones that show up each month. This is where most people go wrong and end up having to use credit cards. Things come up that they weren't prepared for, but could have been. By seeing if you have the money to set aside for the items that don't show up each month, you know if, and by how much, you are living beyond your income.

A lady who came to my workshop was complaining about refinancing her house one year earlier to pay off credit cards. Not only were the balances back, but she was about to be 30 days late on her payments. She was hoping the new refinancing would close before she hurt her credit. When we met individually, she discovered for the first time that when we added in the items that don't show up each month like car repairs, registration fees, and fire insurance, she was spending $425 per month more than she earned. This was an intelligent woman. She was a competent 45-year-old legal secretary in a prestigious law firm, earning over $50,000 a year in 1994. I've even had these experiences with financial planners who were earning $200,000 to $500,000 per year. These concepts and tools apply to every income level.

This method which I call the sophisticated approach happens to be the one my ex-mother-in-law uses. She's actually setting aside the money to replace her roof when it wears out in 15 years. Believe me, it can be done for anything. She started this habit when she was 15 years old with her baby-sitting money. Her dad was a CPA and taught her this method. You and I may not have been as lucky with parent selection.

Personally, I used the more simplified approach to set aside 20% of my income. Each time I deposited money at the bank I transferred 20% into savings. It didn't matter if I was standing in front of the ATM machine or the teller. I received checks for consultations, speaking engagements, book and cassette tape sales, and coaching fees. It didn't matter where the money came from, how large or small the check, 20% was set aside in savings.

My ex-mother-in-law's method is a little too much work for me, but it may not be for you. You may be adept at computer programs like *Microsoft Money* or *Quick Books*. Both my ex-wife and her mother have shown me how to use Quicken, but I can't be bothered. I have my assistant do all of the data entry into Quick Books. I guess in the finance area I'm just a paper and pencil kind of guy.

The Story of Two Attorneys

The following story began in 1991. It's about two attorneys, a husband and wife. At the time the wife came to me she was not practicing law. Her husband asked her to sign a loan to borrow against the equity in their home to pay income taxes that were due. He earned a good living at the time, about $180,000 a year, and was short $15,000 to pay income taxes on April 15. I knew his wife to be a rather quiet type, but in a loud and angry tone she said, "Rennie, I'm sick and tired of this." I was shocked. I asked why she was so upset about this equity loan and she screamed, "It's the third year in a row!" Now I understood her upset. It was the third year in a row of borrowing against the equity in their home to send down the income tax rat hole. (A rat hole refers to a hole in the ground where rats live. If you drop something down in the hole, it's too disgusting to reach in there and retrieve it.)

In the United States we have great opportunities, choices and freedoms that very few countries in the world can match. Our system may not be perfect, but as far as I'm concerned, it's the best there is. To maintain this system, we have an obligation to pay income taxes (among other taxes). If you're not earning any money, you don't pay taxes. If you are earning money you get the privilege to pay taxes that support the country that offers us the freedom to choose to do what we want. These taxes come out of our earnings or profits in business. If we have to pay taxes it means we have made money or profits. It's a fair exchange; taxes for freedom. However, borrowing against a home three years in a row, reducing equity and net worth to pay income taxes is not on my list of suggestions.

When I met with them the first time we filled out the balance sheet and cash flow forms, just like those in the Appendix. We did a lot of guesswork in filling them out. He said he would go to the ATM machine and pull out a couple of hundred dollars, and a few days later it was gone and he didn't know where it went. He said they liked to eat out a lot. Do you think *$600 per month* is a lot to spend eating out? Most of the people in my workshops thought so. And remember, this was $600 in 1991.

Anyway, I asked him to use an earlier version of my *Spending Plan Register*. I didn't have it organized as I do now. I suggested he write down all the money he spent—cash, credit cards or checks—in the *Spending Plan Register*. Or, for checks he wrote, he could use the information from his checkbook register.

Before he even started, he complained it seemed too time consuming. I showed him it would take 5–10 seconds. He asked, "What about 25 cents I might spend in a parking meter?" I said, "Write it down under transportation expense." He asked, "How long do I have to do this?" I told him, "Just six weeks until we get back together." He agreed to use the register.

Six weeks later, we got together and reviewed the data. We looked at what a typical month might look like based on the six weeks he tracked his spending. We had to adjust most of the items either up or down. One of the figures always stands out in my memory. When it came to Meals Out, it was more than he thought. Are you guessing $800 or $1,000 a month instead of $600?

It was actually $1600 a month he was spending eating out. He was ***off by $1,000 per month!*** When you figure he was short $15,000 to pay his taxes, and he was off $1,000 per month on his meals, you can realize he ate practically everything he needed for his taxes. The first year after he used the Spending Plan Register, he saved $12,000 and got current with his income taxes. Not a bad return for a $14 financial tool. What do you think?

In addition, when we got together he had $190,000 of short-term debt: credit cards, business and personal loans. This did not include his home mortgage. Four years later he was still current on his taxes. He reduced his short-term debt by $70,000, leased a new Lexus, and took the whole family on a trip to England, paid in full. Remember I said he was earning $180,000 per year when we first met? Do you want to know what he was earning four years later that produced those dramatic results? It was the same $180,000 a year. He didn't earn a dime more in annual income in four years. The point to this story is this: ***It's not so important how much money you earn; it's what you do with it that makes the difference!***

Six years after our initial meeting, two more things developed. One, all the short-term debt and credit card balances were paid off in full. Two, their family income jumped substantially. What I discovered is that when people handle expenses more responsibly (me included) they seem to generate more income easily and effortlessly.

I have two theories as to how this happens, and you can choose the one that is most comfortable for your belief structure.

First theory: When we have shown we can handle money more responsibly the universe aligns with who we've become and money shows up. We generate money more easily and effortlessly. We see opportunities we would have missed in the past.

Second theory: By taking responsible actions, like paying ourselves first, paying bills on time, or living on less than we earn, we create a psychological shift. We now view ourselves differently. We're proud of who we are. We now make even better choices and decisions. Others recognize this shift in our self image also. We now see opportunities we would have missed before and generate more income easily and effortlessly.

These results have been demonstrated in my life and the lives of my clients over and over again. I don't care which theory you want to adopt, just be sure you adopt one of them. The results prove the actions work. You don't need to understand how electricity works to turn on a switch and have a light come on. You only need to take the action of turning on the switch. You don't need to know why or how paying yourself first will create more money, or how spending less that you earn will create more money. Just do it and you will have the rewards.

Rennie' s Story Continued

Remember when I was bragging about myself and I said I was broke in 1982? Here are the details of where I started on the road to financial independence.

In 1981, my mom died. It was the day after I turned 33. My dad had died when I was 11, so now both my parents were gone. Besides a half-sister on my father's side who lived about 1,000 miles away, all that remained as my closest blood relative was my mom's first son (my half-brother), Larry. I inherited $17,500 and half interest in a four-unit apartment building with Larry. It had profit of about $650 per month. I didn't feel very good about my ability to manage personal finances, so Larry held on to my $325 per month until I needed it.

At the time I was in the pension administration business. I sold and consulted with small corporations all over southern California on qualified retirement plans. This is when I started doing continuing education programs for CPAs and attorneys. I also had some art galleries in California and Arizona. For the four years I had them up to that point, they had doubled in business each year.

When my mom died, I realized I didn't want to be in the pension business and decided to leave effective January 1, 1982. With the $17,500 inheritance and an already existing business, I decided to go into art galleries full time. Well, in 1982 the economy was pretty bad, much like 2009. Businesses were more concerned about paying their phone bills than decorating their offices with art.

By September 1982 I was broke. The $17,500 was long gone. I was another $28,000 in debt on credit cards and business loans. I was three months behind on my mortgage payment and the bank was about to foreclose on my home. I was about to go down the tubes financially. I took soda pop bottles to the grocery store to buy food. I remember I envied the Sparkletts waterman because he had a job, and I didn't have the $14 to pay for the water he delivered. To give you some idea of my intellect: I looked at my situation and figured out what I was doing wasn't working. Smart man, huh?

I decided to get back in the pension business. At least I knew how to make money there. I had ruined my credit by paying 60 and 90 days late, but I was determined to have two things: one, no more consumer debt; and two, not have to work for a living.

I paid off my debts in eighteen months after getting back into the pension business. In 1983, with two other people, we established our own pension administration firm. Again, I did not do this alone, I had two partners, and we had staff. If you recall from the first section of the book on achieving your goals, *allow other people to support you.* I did that and we were able to grow a company quickly and larger than I would have been able to do on my own.

In 1985 my brother died, and I inherited the other half of the apartment building. The profit from the rental income after expenses was now at about $700 per month.

By 1987 our pension company had grown large enough we could sell it, and we did, to a division of a public company.

I went from envying the Sparkletts man in 1982, to having a choice of working or not working in 1987. The things I did, paying myself first, setting long-term goals, not doing it by myself, are the tools I'm sharing with you. I have first-hand knowledge that this stuff works. And if you knew me, you'd know you don't have to be intellectually gifted to do it. I can't even pick out clothes that match.

My next relationship lasted about ten years before my second divorce. If I had taken the advice of my longest-term friend, who was also a divorce attorney, it would not have been as bad as it turned out. I lost half of my assets with the second divorce and had to start over again. At least this time I knew I could rebuild my net worth. I am now in my last and best marriage. We have been together for 16 years, and married for 15. My life is better than ever and I used the concepts in this book to create a multi-million dollar net worth with apartment buildings, starting with $16,000.

I still cannot pick out clothes that match, but I can create a structure to produce financial results, I can ask others for help and support, and I can take action. I bet you can, too. You've already demonstrated that by reading this far. (Even if you haven't filled in the forms, yet.)

The reason I do the UCLA classes, other public workshops, the corporate training, and some individual counseling is to assist other people in creating financial freedom. This is why I created cassette tape programs, CD programs, and books. It can be done and I'm proof of that. Others I have worked with have also proved how powerful these concepts are. And, others don't have to go through what I went through.

Step 12.

Create a Prosperous Financial Future

This book is designed to assist people to create the savings so they will have something to invest. Now that you are paying yourself first, you can create a prosperous financial future by putting that money to work. How? That's what's next

The following sections will show you how easy it is to begin investing by educating you on the very basics. I hope this is of interest to you and I present it in a way that makes it easy to understand and compelling enough for you to take action on NOW. All of the other information in this book was to get you to this point. This is where, or how, financial freedom is created. It is not achieved just from spending less, getting out of debt, or making better purchasing decisions. Financial freedom is created by taking the money you saved and investing it to produce a stream of income so you no longer have to work. This is where you have money working for you, instead of you working for money. If you find this section does not provide enough information, check out one of the many books available at your local bookstore or library.

Simple Interest

Most of the time when you save or invest your money, it will be earning at a compounded rate that I will explain later. You want to avoid simple interest earnings. This is an old and rare way of paying interest on borrowed money. I'm bringing this up just in case this is offered to you as a way of paying you for money you loan to someone, or deposit somewhere. It works like this: You deposit $100 in a bank which pays simple interest at the rate of 5% per year. At the end of the first year you would receive $5, and at the end of the second year, another $5, and so on. If you let all of the interest add up, at the end of 10 years your account would have a total of $150. This represents the $100 you deposited plus 10 years of $5 per year, $50 ($5 x 10 yrs. = $50.)

Compound interest pays on your deposit and on your interest each compounding period—which could be annually, monthly, or even daily. Using the same example as above, with $100 compounding annually at 5% it would look like this: At the end of the first year you would receive $5. At the end of year two you would receive $5.25, and by year 10 it would be $7.75. This is $2.25 more than a simple interest calculation. Do not underestimate this important concept because I'm using small numbers. The concept works the same with large numbers, too.

The account value at the end of ten years from *compound* interest would be $168.88 instead of $150. At the end of 30 years, $100 at *simple* interest would grow to $250. Compound would produce $432.19, which is 73% more money! Instead of using $100 as an example, let's use $100,000. The *difference* would be $182,000 more from compound interest than from simple interest. This is based on a 30-year timeframe, at the same 5% interest rate.

The Magic of Compound Earnings

Let's move on to the *magic* of compound earnings. Note: I used the word earnings instead of interest. I just explained compound *interest* in the previous section, and now I'm using the world *earnings*. Many people are not aware of the difference, so I'm going to review it. *Interest* refers to the income an individual, a bank, corporation or the government pays you when you loan them money. Interest is only one component of earnings. *Earnings* represent two components: the interest or dividends which are paid, plus the *growth in value* of a stock, bond, real estate, or any investment. This is also called *total return*. Many people are led astray by advertising that illustrates investment earnings from the past that are total return figures. You are already aware a bank or bond pays interest. People see a mutual fund advertise it earned 24% in a previous year and they think this means the fund paid investors 24% interest. This is just based on a lack of education. No one was paid 24% interest. Investors may have received a 2% dividend distribution and the balance represented a 22% increase in the value of their shares.

In addition to a lack of education, when I work with groups, whether it's a class of four people, or a presentation to 400, there are attitudes people express that concern me. It relates to a study I read about several years ago. People were asked, "What would you do with $5,000 received as a gift?" Many of them said they would pay off some debts or bills, buy a new car or entertainment center. The point is that had plenty of places to spend the money. When the question was asked, "What would you do with $50,000 (assuming it had no tax obligations)?" They answered more along the lines of spending a little bit, but putting most of into some savings or investment where it could grow in value.

The study showed most people would spend what they perceive to be a small amount of money, and only look to save or invest larger amounts. The fallacy is you can't get to the larger amounts if spend all the small amounts. You must also have respect for small amounts of money.

Look at the next chart. If you spend $5 today, you probably wouldn't even miss it. That's probably not enough money to buy a cup of coffee and a muffin at Starbucks. If you saved $5 per day, you probably wouldn't miss that either. If you earned a 10%

return on it, you'd have close to $114,000 in 20 years. Of that $114,000, only $36,000 represents the $5 per day. The $78,000 difference is all earnings. This is the *magic of compound earnings*. Money over time creates geometric growth. Start now, even if it's with little bits of money.

Here is what $5 per day at 10% will do:

2 years	$3,967
5 years	$11, 616
10 years	$30, 727
20 years	$113,905

($5/day = $36,000) Earnings =　$77, 905

30 years	$339,073

($5/day = $54,000) Earnings =　$285, 703

Some people tell me, "You can't get 10% in the bank." I didn't say to put it in the bank. I said 10% earnings, not interest. Remember my description of interest versus earnings? If you don't, just go back a few paragraphs. The following paragraph uses some numbers to illustrate the difference.

If you have a savings account that pays 5% annual interest on a $1,000 balance, you would receive $50 for the year. (Someday we may get back to these rates.) If you had a $1,000, 5% government bond and interest rates dropped, the bond would become more valuable. Let's say it increased in value by $100. If you held it for one year and sold it, you would have received $50 in interest and $100 in gain, for a total of $150. This means you earned 15% on your $1,000 investment (150 ÷ 1,000 = .15 = 15%). I want to make this clear, because you will not earn the level of return I'm using in my example by having money sit in the bank. You will need to make investments.

You could buy some real estate, stocks, bonds, or mutual funds, which I will be describing later on.

The Rule of 72

This is a shorthand method to calculate how long it takes money to double based on the earnings percentage. If you divide 72 by an interest rate or earnings rate, you will find the years it will take for money to double in value. If you divide 72 by the numbers of years someone says it will take for the money to double, you will be able to calculate the earnings.

$$\frac{72}{\text{Earnings rate}} = \text{Years for money to double}$$

$$\frac{72}{\text{Yrs. to double}} = \text{Earnings rate needed/received}$$

As an example, if I told you your money would double in 18 years and you divided that in 72, you would have a 4% earnings rate. If I said you would earn 12%, your money would double in 6 years. What's this rule used for? Doing a quick calculation in your head or on paper when you don't have a calculator handy.

Become a Millionaire on $10 per day - Even with Debts!

The following is another perspective on the "pay yourself first" approach. It's difficult for me to contain my excitement when I look at what's possible with systematic long-term investing. You do not have to be a savvy investor to create a million-dollar portfolio. It can be done with as little as $10 per day, earning 12% over 30 years. There are mutual funds with track records of 20, 30 and 40 years with returns in excess of 12% on an annual compounded rate. I am not going to go into sophisticated investment strategies, but I will show you how to invest in an easy way, a secure way, a way which will allow you to get better returns than the bank or government bonds, and be able to sleep at night. Obviously, nothing is guaranteed, but then there is no guarantee we will rise from bed tomorrow either.

Here's an inspirational calculation: If you pay yourself first 10% of your current income and invest it at 12% earnings, compounding annually for 20 years, you will create enough invested assets which could pay out close to 100% of your current income, and not reduce the assets. In 30 years, you would produce a portfolio with enough invested assets to pay yourself 350% of your current income!

Let's demonstrate this by way of an example: If you earned $3,000 per month, which is $36,000 per year, (I'm keeping things simple and not factoring in taxes) and *paid yourself first* 10%, which would be $300 per month, or $10 per day, and invested this and earned 12% per year, you would have an investment portfolio of $1,048,500 in 30 years. What's $10 per day? It's pocket change. It's a couple of caffé lattes and a muffin from Starbucks. It's a first-run movie ticket if you can get free parking. It's renting four videos. It's dry cleaning three pairs of slacks. It's money you don't think is significant enough to invest. If you're willing to invest pocket change, you can create financial freedom.

This million-dollar portfolio would be able to provide you with an income close to $126,000 per year. As long as you continued to earn 12% on your portfolio, this $126,000 could be paid out year after year for as long as you lived. This is more than three times your annual income of $36,000. If you took out something less that what the portfolio was earning, it would continue to grow in size and could produce a larger income over time. Paying yourself 10% of your $3,000 per month income and investing it can produce passive investment earnings of $10,500 per month, or 350% more than your $3,000 per month income. Over the 30 years, you would have invested $108,000 and produced $1,048,500. That's almost 10 times what you put in! From an investment of $10 per day you could create an income of $350 per day. (35 times what you put in!) This is the power of investing over time at compound earnings. The stock market will rise, and it will fall, but over any 10 year period of time the direction of growth is up.

Thirty years is not a long time. I don't know how old you are, but think about what you may have been doing ten, twenty, or thirty years ago and consider how fast it went by. If thirty years seems too long, look over Chart 1. You will see at twenty years your investment could grow by more than four times what you put in.

Chart 1: $10 per day at 12% earnings
($300 per month)

Years	Money In	Account Value	Ratio of account value to what you put in
10	$ 36,000	$ 69,000	almost 2 times
20	$ 72,000	$ 297,000	more than 4 times
30	$108,000	$1,048,500	almost 10 times

Also, notice in the chart the geometric progression of money growing over time due to the compounding. The longer you do it, the more dramatic the return becomes. To take advantage of the compounding effect, you must start now!

The next two concepts are revolutionary. Other financial planners or accountants may talk about the cost of waiting to invest, but I've not come across anyone speaking about what happens if you invest when you have debt.

As you can see from Chart 1, you must start now to take advantage of earnings compounding over time. You might ask, "But what if I have debt? Shouldn't I pay that off first?" The answer is NO! You can see that clearly from Chart 2. If you waited as little as two years to pay off your debt before you begin investing, it hurts your investment return far more than any interest you would save. In Chart 1 you would have $1,048,500 at the end of 30 years. In Chart 2, which shows a delay of investing for two years, you would have $819,000 after another 28 years. This is a loss of $229,000, just for waiting two years to begin. This lost money could generate an additional income of $27,500 per year. This is enough money for a couple to leave the United States twice per year for the rest of their lives on a two-week European vacation and stay in "5 Star" hotels. I also have a section titled, "Don't Pay Off Your Debts First" which offers more on this point of view.

Chart 2: Pay off debt in two years and then begin to invest

Assumes a debt of $6,000 paid off at $300 per month, (18% interest). Annual interest, $1,080.

Yrs	Money In	New Acct. Value	Instead of	Difference*	Interest saved
10	$ 36,000	$ 48,000	$ 69,000	$ 21,000	$ 8,640
20	$ 72,000	$227,000	$ 297,000	$ 70,000	$19,440
30	$108,000	$819,500	$1,048,500	$229,000	$30,240

*Difference reflects two years of less money contributed into the investment account plus lost earnings.

What if the debt was never paid off, but interest payments were made, year in and year out? It would still be less than the lost earnings from waiting to invest. In year 30, you would have $229,000 more money by starting two years earlier to invest. How can this difference be so dramatic? This is because the earnings from your investment are compounding, but the interest on your loan is at simple interest. If you forgot about the difference, go back and review simple interest and compound earnings. The point is this: you must not wait to begin paying yourself first and investing. Look at Chart 3 - you must START NOW.

When my son was 26 years old. He already had $12,000 invested, and he only got paid $25,000 per year through his job. He'd been earning about 16% for the last several years on his account (he had chosen some aggressive mutual funds), but even if he were earning 12%, if he just added $2,000 per year ($39 per week) to that amount until he's age 65, he would have

$2,365,000. He is now 42, married with 2 children and has several hundred thousand dollars.

Chart 3: If debt never paid off
  ($6,000 debt at 18%, annual interest, $1,080)

Years	Interest paid	Difference*	Benefit
10	$10,800	$ 21,000	$ 10,200
20	$21,600	$ 70,000	$ 51,400
30	$32,400	$229,000	$196,600

*from Chart 2

The best part is this: I've not taken into consideration that as your income grows, you can make larger investment deposits. If you pay yourself 10% of $3,000 per month, you invest $300. If your income grows to $4,000 per month, the 10% is now $400 per month. Your income will grow over time, won't it?

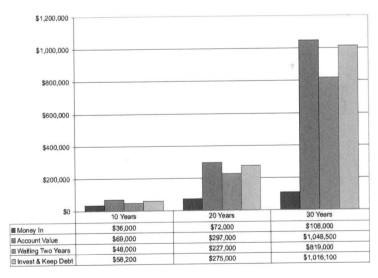

	10 Years	20 Years	30 Years
■ Money In	$36,000	$72,000	$108,000
■ Account Value	$69,000	$297,000	$1,048,500
■ Waiting Two Years	$48,000	$227,000	$819,000
▢ Invest & Keep Debt	$58,200	$275,000	$1,016,100

Please recognize I am not encouraging you to keep debt. The emphasis of this book is to support you in paying off your debt and becoming financially free. What I am showing you in Chart 3 is the value of beginning to invest now, regardless of your debt. If you never pay it off, but start investing now, you can create financial prosperity. In addition to the financial rewards, as I've said before, paying yourself first creates psychological advantages also, which can support you in paying off your debt more easily.

I hope you see the sense in starting to invest now—and you can start with as little as $100. Your next question might be, "How?" Whether $100 or $10,000, you would still start in the same place. Following this section, I will go into some specific strategies. Meanwhile, here are some suggestions on how to get started:

- Continue to educate yourself by taking classes at a local college or university extension program. Go to the library, bookstore or Amazon and get other books on investing where the book relates to your investment stage or experience. Read the business section of any major metropolitan newspaper or get the Wall Street Journal.
- Join an investment club. For information on investment clubs, you can find books in the library or bookstore, or write to: National Association of Investors Corporation at P.O. Box 220, Royal Oak, MI 48068, and see the section on "How to Invest Without Paying Commissions" for more alternatives.

- Go to a financial planner. Many will only work with people who can invest lots of money. Many, however, especially those who are young or new in the business, will work with those who are just starting to invest. Many don't even charge a fee, they work with you on the basis that you will buy the products (stocks, bonds, insurance) from them, and they will earn a commission from that. For help in choosing one, read the upcoming section, "How to Pick a Financial Planner."
- Go to a full-service broker to help you, if there are any left after the financial market meltdown of 2008 when we

lost Bear Stearns and Lehman Brothers. Full-service brokers charge the highest level of commissions and provide advice and research. Ask several people you trust, who are investing, to give you some recommendations or referrals. Again, see the section "How to Pick a Financial Planner."

- Go to a discount broker, like TD Ameritrade, Scottrade, or E-Trade, and you can buy one share of stock at its current market price plus about $20 to cover the transaction costs. A discount broker does not provide research or advice. You could also go to Charles Schwab, which is halfway between a full-service broker and a discount broker. Again, refer to the section "How to Pick a Financial Planner."

- Use a computer. If you don't have access to the Internet, go to your library. There is a world of information available to you there, plus computers. One very popular site, motleyfool.com, has loads of information on how to get started and different simple strategies to use in selecting stocks. Also, see the upcoming sections "Dogs of the Dow" and "How to Invest Without Paying Commissions" for more information.

- If you've been unable to get the support or direction you need from your family, friends, co-workers or the recommendations I've made here, feel free to call my office for a telephone consultation. I care about the progress of my readers. Short calls (10 minutes) are free but I do charge for longer consulting calls.

Investing versus Gambling

When I speak about investments or investing in the market, I'm referring to purchasing items like quality corporate stocks, not gambling. There is a difference. Many people go to Las Vegas or Atlantic City to gamble, have fun and be entertained. The stock market can be approached the same way. However, I am NOT suggesting playing the market when I speak about investments.

Yes, you can have fun and you can be entertained from your stock market investment portfolio. However, I do NOT speak about *playing* the market or *gambling* in the market when addressing clients about investing. Playing the market and investing do not belong in the same sentence. They do not mean the same thing.

You can gamble in Las Vegas, but unless you own the casino, take advantage of neighborhood conditions or take advantage of gamblers, you can't invest while in Las Vegas. Gambling or playing the market is not the same as investing in the market. How can you gamble in the market? You can bet on the rise or fall of a stock or the market itself. You can bet that certain things may happen by certain dates. Gambling has names like puts, calls, straddles, options, butterflies and derivatives. I've heard people say they're not gambling when they buy a put or call., They say they're hedging. Well, that's what gamblers do; they hedge their bets.

Another form of gambling is to use the concept of momentum investing. You buy and sell (trade) stocks on a moment by moment basis, taking advantage of price fluctuations due to economic conditions, government actions or investor psychology. You can spend three to four hours daily on a home computer involved in this approach of active trading. If you would like to know more I suggest the book *Wall Street Money Machine* by Wade B. Cook. Although he has been indicted and found guilty based on his business practices you will understand the concept from his book. I am not recommending this approach any more than I would recommend you become a professional poker player, but if that's what's in your blood, if that approach matches your value system, then go for it.

How does gambling pay off? Just like in Las Vegas you lose most of the time, unless you're a professional. When you win, you can win big with a small bet. This is like roulette when the little ball lands on the number you chose. It looks the same when you gamble in the stock market; a little bet can pay off big.

Unfortunately, gambling and investing have been tied together since the early 1900s. Even the term that represents the largest most stable corporations, Blue Chips, is said to get its expression from the most valuable poker chips, which are blue.

I did enough gambling in my business. I gambled that my education, training and experience would pay off. I spent thousands of dollars publishing another book and it might not sell. I could have asked, "Will I make the level of profit I project on my cassette tape program?" If I fly to some city to sign up another corporate training client, will it go smoothly? Or, might there be unexpected delays or breakdowns? Since it feels like I gambled enough in my business, when it came to the stock market, I invested - I did not gamble.

Most of my money (90%) is in real estate. This is based on my attitudes and values. How did I invest in the stock market? I purchased the stock of companies that had a track record of growing dividends and share price increases. I bought them, reviewed them once per year, and continued to hold them if they continued to meet the criteria I established. By 2001, when the .com bubble burst and people were losing 30-40% of the value of their holdings, I was earning 1%. For more information on how to choose those companies I suggest you read *America's Finest Companies Investment Plan* by Bill Staton. You can also read *The Motley Fool Investment Guide* by David and Tom Gardner, or get their information online at www.motleyfool.com. While I don't agree with everything they recommend, there are many basic truths to the investing approach they take. I'll go over one of the simple strategies in a section after I describe the "Dow." It's called the "Dogs of the Dow" approach.

How to Pick a Financial Planner

Again, this is not something you have to do on your own. When I want to discuss some financial planning ideas, I speak to someone I can trust. This doesn't have to be some high profile financial planner, and I know many of them around the country because of my activities in the past.

How do you find someone you can trust? Ask. Ask other people you trust for referrals. Perhaps you know, or have, a CPA, attorney, bank officer, successful business owner or wealthy friend. Ask someone who may be familiar with a particular planner's work, abilities and specialty.

The Financial Planning Association (FPANET.org), Certified Financial Planner Board (CFP.net) and National Association of Personal Financial Advisors (NAPFA.org) all have "find an adviser" tools plus other hiring tips.

It is often best to speak with three planners you are considering. When you meet, ask them questions to see if there's a match for you. Regardless of the credentials or background of a financial planner, don't abdicate your responsibility to oversee what is going on. You need to continue to question recommendations and be skeptical about the planner's suggestions. You need to educate yourself on the particulars in any decision. Would it make sense to go to a travel agent to plan a vacation and say, "I've got $10,000. Send me somewhere."? Of course not. You must be actively involved in the process. To assist in thinking clearly, breathe deep and take in oxygen. It's one of the American Medical Association recommended daily nutritional requirements.

Here are some questions you can use to interview someone you're considering:

1. What is your background, education and experience?
2. How do you stay current with changes in your field?
3. How do you get paid? What conflicts could arise between your interests and mine?
4. I am most concerned about _____. How might you handle that?
5. What are the typical circumstances and incomes of the clients with whom you work?
6. Are there others to whom you refer that assist you with your recommendations?
7. Are they in your office?

8. Do you get assistance for help in complex areas of tax planning, portfolio management, insurance evaluation or estate planning?
9. Can I see a sample of your work?
10. Do you fully disclose commissions you will earn if you sell products?
11. If you don't sell financial products, can you make specific recommendations on how I can buy them at the best price?
12. What continuing services do you provide? How much do they cost?
13. Have you been reprimanded or disciplined by regulatory or industry bodies? Can you provide their phone numbers so I can verify that?

Stocks

Stocks, shares, shares of stock and equities refer to the same thing. They represent units of ownership in a corporation. Any of the products you buy or use were probably manufactured, distributed or sold by some corporation. If the corporation is doing a good job and making profits it could be a good business to own, and you may be able to own a part of it, if it's a public company. A private company cannot be purchased by the general public. This is also called closely held stock. The way to own part of a public company is to purchase shares of stock that the company issues and offers for sale. It is usually purchased through a stock exchange, like the New York, American, Pacific, or Nasdaq. Some companies will sell directly to the public and you can read about that under the heading, "How to Invest Without Paying Commissions." This information is also available in Staton's book *America's Finest Companies*, which I mentioned earlier.

Bonds

Bonds are issued by a corporation or government entity. A

bond represents a promise to pay for money borrowed. Interest is paid to the lender, who is the bondholder. This can be an individual or other organization that loans the money. The face amounts are often issued at $1,000, $5,000 or $10,000 amounts per bond. Interest rates are higher than bank interest and increase based on the risk involved, or the ability of the borrower to repay the loan. The term *junk bonds* refer to bonds issued by companies where the risk of default is high. Maturity dates are often 10 years or longer. Interest is paid during the maturity period and the amount loaned is repaid at the end of the period.

The value of the bond can rise or fall, based on changes in the interest rates available in the general market place. If you have a bond that pays 10% interest, and new bonds are issued which have rates at 8%, the value of the 10% bond will rise above its face amount. This excess over the face amount is called a *premium*. Bonds do not have to be held by the owner to maturity, they can be sold earlier and fetch more or less money than the face amount depending on changes in interest rates. (If you would like more education on bonds, there are several excellent books available at your local library, bookstore or Amazon.)

The Dow

You've heard it on the evening news, you hear it on the radio while you commute, if often makes front-page headlines, and you may not know what it is. It's the "Dow." This is the term often used for the Dow Jones Industrial Average, also called the Dow 30 Industrials. This is the most frequently quoted index which lists the prices of one share of stock from 30 household names such as Disney, McDonald's, Coca-Cola, and so on. It is supposedly designed to measure the health of the economy based on the products manufactured and sold by these corporations. Its validity as an accurate gauge of the economy is widely debated and many of the companies listed are not even in manufacturing, unless you consider movies and hamburgers manufactured products.

The following charts list the companies on the Dow as of September 1997 and eleven years later in October 2008. The companies on the list have changed over the years, which also detracts from the ability to accurately gauge numerical changes in the index over time. In addition, in 1997 the prices were quoted in fractions, such as Coca-Cola at 80 5/8, which would be $80.625. By 2000 this was changed to real dollar and cent denominations.

As an example of the company changes, in August of 1999, Union Carbide, which had been on the Dow since 1928, was to be acquired by Dow Chemical, which is not on the Dow. This means a slot opened up for another company to be listed that was chosen by the editors of the Wall Street Journal. They have the right to decide who will and won't be listed on the Dow. Another change on the list occurred when Travelers Insurance bought Citicorp. The Dow used to be limited only to corporations who had issues traded on the New York Stock Exchange. Corporations like Intel and Microsoft, among the country's largest corporations, were not on the list until 1999 because their issues were traded on the Nasdaq.

The concept behind the Dow is as follows: If we look at the value reported on 2/21/96 (not shown), you could add the price of one share of stock from each of the thirty corporations and it would total 5458.53. (Stock prices are quoted without a "$" symbol.) That final number also includes an adjustment of each share of stock calculating its worth based on how much money the total corporation is worth. This is the number you would have heard in the news that evening, or printed in the paper the following day.

On August 5, 1999, the index was at 10,674.77. This is an increase of 95% over a three-and-half-year period, representing a 21% annual compounded rate of return, more than four times the interest from a bank savings account. This was a very strong period of growth in the market, as measured by the Dow. By October 2007 the Dow reached 13,930. By October 2008 it was down to 8,379, a decline of 40% in one year. On May 21, 2014 it was at 16,533.06. Volatility exists.

Disclaimer: This listing of stocks is not an offer to sell securities. This listing has not been approved by any government agency. Securities may only be offered through a current prospectus. All investments are subject to certain risks. For example, those that include common stocks are affected by fluctuating stock prices. No investment advice is being offered through this list. Registered Investment Advisory services can be offered through securities representatives of a registered broker/dealer.

Dow Jones Industrial Average Stocks
October 24, 2008   http://money.cnn.com/data/dow30/

1. 3M	59.61
2. Alcoa	9.41
3. American Express	24.05
4. AT&T	24.68
5. Bank of America	21.07
6. Boeing	45.24
7. Caterpillar	33.30
8. Chevron	63.91
9. Citigroup	12.14
10. Coca Cola	41.61
11. du Pont	29.33
12. Exxon-Mobil	69.04
13. General Electric	17.83
14. General Motors	5.95
15. Hewlett-Packard	32.44
16. IBM	82.07
17. Home Depot	18.51
18. Intel	14.28
19. Johnson & Johnson	60.79
20. JP Morgan & Chase	35.43
21. Kraft Foods	27.10
22. McDonalds	53.06
23. Merck & Co	27.35
24. Microsoft	21.96

25. Pfizer	16.57	
26. Procter & Gamble	58.87	
27. United Technologies	47.31	
28. Verizon Communications	25.08	
29. Wal-Mart	51.40	
30. Walt Disney	22.61	
	8,378.95	

September 25, 1997

1. Allied Signal	42 3/4
2. Alcoa	80 11/16
3. American Express	81 1/4
4. AT&T	45 1/16
5. Boeing	54 5/8
6. Caterpillar	54 3/16
7 Chevron	84 9/16
8. Coca-Cola	80 5/8 (80.625)
9. Disney	78 11/16
10. du Pont	62 3/4
11. Eastman Kodak	61 5/8
12. Exxon	64 3/16
13. General Electric	68 5/8
14. General Motors	66 3/8
15. Goodyear	67 3/4
16. Hewlett-Packard	71 1/2
17. IBM	101 9/16
18. International Paper	53 1/2
19. Johnson & Johnson	58 5/8
20. McDonald's	48 9/16
21. Merck	101 1/4
22. J.P. Morgan	115 1/2
23. Philip Morris	41 13/16
24. Proctor & Gamble	68 15/16
25. Sears, Roebuck	56 3/4
26. Travelers Group	69 7/16
27. 3M	87.0
28. ~~Union Carbide~~ (acquired by Dow Chemical 8/99)	

29. United Technologies	82 7/8
30. Wal-Mart	36 11/16
	7,848.01

The Dogs of the Dow

I'm not certain of the origin of this investing term. It may come from sled dogs that lead the pack, or dogs that lag behind. The "Dogs of the Dow" generally refers to 10 stocks of the 30 listed on the Dow Jones Industrials. They have a price per share that lags behind other stocks on the Dow, when viewed by corporation's earnings per share. It would be expected that these ten stocks would grow in share price faster than the other stocks on the Dow, to reflect an alignment of its value based on its earnings.

The strategy is based on the calculation that you can beat the market return, based on the Dow, by limiting your investment portfolio to 10 of the stocks that are expected to be the best performing from the Dow index. It makes sense the rate of return will be higher from the best ten performers on the index, than the performance of the entire 30 stocks listed. You can even beat this return by focusing on the top four or five stocks from the average. Again, these are major corporations that will most likely still be in business when you and I are dust. We are not talking gambling here. You can invest in a mutual fund that is patterned after this concept through many of the major stock brokerage firms. See the section "Mutual Funds" for a general explanation of this investment approach.

You can also create this on your own. The information on which stocks make up the "Dogs" can be obtained by calling a stock brokerage firm, depending on who is left standing after the meltdown in 2008, or go to www.dogsofthedow.com to see an updated list. Another would be www.motleyfool.com. When I first wrote this section in 1998, the top 10 stocks were: Philip Morris, AT&T, Caterpillar, International Paper, Exxon, Kodak, General Motors, Chevron, 3M and J.P. Morgan. In 2008 the following companies were on the list: Citigroup, GM, Pfizer,

AT&T, JP Morgan Chase, Altria, Verizon, DuPont and Home Depot. In 2013 the following companies were on the list: AT&T, Verizon, Intel, Merck, Pfizer, DuPont, Hewlett-Packard, General Electric, McDonald's, and Johnson & Johnson

Once you've made your purchase, you do NOT have to look in the newspaper daily to see how you are doing. You only need to review your portfolio once per year. At that time you can see which stocks to keep, sell, or just invest in the new leaders. Keep it simple. Limit your portfolio to 5–8 stocks. If you want to do some gambling, you can add a stock or two from a speculative area for a total portfolio of 10 holdings.

Remember when I was showing you how little bits of money add up to large amounts? You don't need a lot of money to get started in building your portfolio. You can start with as little as $100, or even less. You can go to a discount broker, such as TDAmeritrade, or Scottrade, and purchase one share of stock at its market price plus a small transaction fee. You can even buy stocks on the Internet through places like E*TRADE at a lower transaction fee. I heard a funny observation from Charles Schwab regarding people trading online by themselves instead of using a broker. He said, "It allows people to make the same investment blunders as before, only faster."

In a new book by Michael Lewis, *Flash Boys: A Wall Street Revolt*, the author contends that the stock market is rigged, like this would be news to the average investor. What is news is how it is rigged in favor of the large trading firms that use high speed computer trading. They have literally figured out the shortest route to an exchange over the Internet to shave fractions of milliseconds so that they are able to identify your desire to buy shares of a company and buy them in front of you and sell them back to you at a higher price. This might only give them an advantage of a few pennies, but with millions of trades this amounts to billions of dollars in a year. What does that mean to you? It might mean that you paid an extra $1 to buy 100 shares of a stock. When you look at this that way, it's not really very relevant to the average investor. But it does confirm that the big boys will take advantage of the small investors.

Before you start however, you will need to have established your future spending account for the expense items we discussed earlier, like car repairs, property taxes, vacations, clothing and so on which don't show up each month. The spending account money will not be invested; it will be sitting in a savings (spending) account ready for the time when you need it.

How to Invest Without Paying Commissions

Over 200 companies in the U.S. and around the world offer the opportunity to investors to purchase their stock without going through stockbrokers and paying commissions. They vary from consumer products to utilities. Some very well-known names are on the list, such as Gillette, Mattel, Chevron, Exxon, Merck, Owens Corning, Home Depot, and McDonald's.

You can buy direct for a little as $50 to $1,000. Most often, dividends can go back in and purchase additional shares. This is called a dividend re-investment program, or DRIP. If you want to know more you can request a free list of the stocks by writing to DRIP Investor, 7412 Calumet Ave., #200, Hammond, IN 46324-2692.

You can find a more complete list ay NetStock Direct (http://netstockdirect.com.) You still need to read the prospectus or plan documents to make sure the fees aren't out of line. But even with the fees, it could be less to buy a no-load stock than purchase through a broker. You may still want to use a broker or financial planner after you read the section, "Don't be Afraid of a Load."

Investment Clubs

Many people enjoy the opportunity to meet and discuss their investment ideas and get feedback from like-minded people. There are many different approaches and personalities to investment clubs as there are people.

Some clubs do extensive research based on fundamentals, others go on hunches with minimal research, and still others will buy and hold while others trade actively. Some will go for the stocks of large corporations and others want start-ups. Some require $25 per month to participate; others could require $1,000 up front.

To find out more about investment clubs, you can find books written by some clubs: *The Beardstown Ladies' Common Sense Guide* and *The Money Club* by Crockett and Felenstein are two examples. Do not believe the specifics about their profits, they are bragging. Just look at the big picture – working together. The leading source of information is the National Association of Investors Corporation. This is the organization that oversees investment clubs nationally. The NAIC's web address is www.better-investing.org .

Mutual Funds

Mutual funds allow you to participate in the investment opportunities offered by the stock, bond and money markets, with several advantages over trying to build your own portfolio of individual stocks. Mutual funds offer these four advantages:

Diversification. You can invest in a broad variety of stocks, bonds, and other securities with as little as $250. This helps reduce the risks of investing.

Professional Management. Experienced managers and analysts invest your money. They study companies, industry forecasts, and market factors before (and after) committing to an investment.

Various objectives. You can pursue a variety of objectives with mutual funds, from seeking high income to long-term growth, from technology stocks to forest products, from conservative to aggressive investors.

Liquidity. You can withdraw your money at any time at the current net asset value, which may be higher or lower than your purchase price.

Funds that pay a sales commission to the person who provides you the fund are called *load funds*. A 'load' is a commission. *No-load funds* do not pay sales commissions. Both load and no-load funds will still charge management fees. These and other details are found in the prospectus that the companies must provide to you before you invest. Please read this information. You can get a list of various load and no-load funds by calling Mutual Fund Forecaster (800) 442-9000 and asking for a free sample of their newsletter.

Don't Be Afraid of a Load

While I briefly discussed in previous sections how to buy stocks without paying commissions, and that you can purchase mutual funds with or without loads (commissions), you don't have to be afraid of paying a commission or load. All mutual funds will have various management fees and expense charges, whether or not they charge a load. These costs are usually deducted from the overall fund and are reflected in a reduced rate of return. They are not taken out of your individual account. If you have little investment experience, you may want to look at the load from the perspective of paying a fee for a service. And, you could actually be financially better off paying a commission. I'll explain this later with a chart, but for now let's look at how you might see a commission, or load, from the perspective of simply paying for a fee for service.

If you are someone who repairs your own car, then you probably wouldn't pay a mechanic to change your oil. If you can do it yourself, and it's something you normally do, why pay someone else? You may have taken classes, read books, played around on your own, or been taught by someone else how to repair a car.

Over the years, I've spoken to thousands of people in seminars, and most people I speak with don't repair their own cars. And, none of them take their auto in for repair and expect the mechanic to do it for free. The mechanic has the training, education and experience to do the repair, and people expect to pay for that.

If you have the education, training and experience to do financial planning, insurance analysis or investment evaluations, then you wouldn't need to use a financial planner, insurance agent or stockbroker. If you can do it yourself, you wouldn't need to pay someone else for their advice or assistance, unless you still want to have someone confirm your conclusions. You've probably heard the expression, "If a lawyer represents himself (or herself) in court, they have a fool for a client."

If you want someone who can provide advice, someone who can ask you questions which will create clarity and provide appropriate recommendations based on your unique situation, then you will need to pay someone either through a fee, or through a commission from the products they sell. As I said in a previous section, many financial planners and insurance agents will work with you for only the commissions they will receive from the products you buy. This can be an easy, nearly painless way, to get advice and pay for their services.

Now, let's look at the chart for some hard evidence on why you don't have to fear paying a load. I've used two mutual funds as an example. I've tracked the management fees and expenses shown from the prospectus of each one. The prospectus is the document that is required to be provided to you under law. It contains the information that the Securities and Exchange Commission feels every investor ought to have. Always read the prospectus and, if you don't understand what it says, have it explained to you. One of the funds is from one of the largest mutual fund companies in the country and represents the no-load column. The information for the load column comes from another of the country's largest fund that most financial planners and insurance agents represent. The chart illustrates that if you're going to buy a mutual fund, and keep it for only a couple of years, you'd be better off buying a no-load fund. If you are going to keep the fund for five years or more, you may be better off in a fund where you pay a commission up front. You would want to look up this information for yourself with specific numbers for any of the funds you are considering.

I've also made some assumptions for the chart. One, both funds have the same rate of return over the period shown, and there is no way to know if this will happen. The rate of return for the future is calculated the same as the past performance, and there are no guarantees this will occur. Second, the management fees and expenses remain level throughout the period. In reality, these items could increase or decrease. These fees can be higher or lower from one mutual fund company to another, and even from one fund to another within a family of funds. As an example, Fidelity has dozens of mutual funds available and each one can have different expense and management fees.

The total expenses that would reduce your return include the commission paid to the salesperson and their firm plus the management fees and expense charges. This is shown under the load column and in the first year adds up to 7.34%. In the no-load column, which represents management and expense fees alone, with no commissions, this figure is only 2.62%. However, you'll notice the expense fees in the load column are less than those in the no-load column and, over time, this makes a big difference. By the fifth year, the total expenses, including the load for the load column, are 12.30%, while the no-load column total expenses are 13.10%.

Chart: (Please read the text for an explanation of this chart)

LOAD				NO-LOAD	
Year	Comm.	Expense Charges	Total	Expense Charges	Total
1	6.1%	+1.24%	= 7.34%	2.62%	= 2.62%
2	-0-	+1.24	= 8.58	2.62	= 5.24
3	-0-	+1.24	= 9.82	2.62	= 7.86
4	-0-	+1.24	= 11.06	2.62	= 10.48
5	-0-	+1.24	= 12.30	2.62	= 13.10
6	-0-	+1.24	= 13.54	2.62	= 15.72
7	-0-	+1.24	= 14.78	2.62	= 18.34
8	-0-	+1.24	= 16.02	2.62	= 20.96

This chart is showing you that by the fifth year, you will have paid less in this load mutual fund than in the no-load fund to which it is compared. By the eighth year, the difference is over 4% more paid in the no-load fund than if you had stayed in the load fund. So, if you are going to keep your money invested in the same mutual fund for several years, you don't have to be afraid of a load. And, by paying a load, you should have been given the advice about which fund would best suit your attitude and objectives. With several thousand funds from which to choose, that can be an intelligent and time-saving approach to selecting the right one.

Dollar-Cost Averaging

This is a method of systematic investing. It requires an investor to purchase equal dollar amounts of stock, or a mutual fund, on a regular basis, such as weekly, monthly, quarterly, etc. The success of the strategy is based on the fact that the same amount of money will buy a different amount of shares based on prices rising or falling with market conditions. The strategy alleviates investment timing problems. While no specialized expertise is required for success, it does require the discipline to invest regularly, even in declining markets. Over time, this approach yields an average cost of shares that is less than the average price. Over time, investments at a lower share price will benefit your account when you ultimately sell. It is better to dollar-cost average in a falling market than to make lump sum investments. This also works well when you are nervous about current holdings. In a mutual fund, if you re-invest dividends and capital gains in additional fund shares, you are using a type of dollar-cost averaging.

Insurance

There have been too many books written about various types of insurance for me to take up the time and space to go into any detail on that subject here. What I will do is repeat the reason for purchasing this product, which I used when I discussed risk

159

management as one of the six roadblocks to financial independence: Insurance is used to protect yourself in the areas where you can't afford to do it on your own. If you have a small fender bender and there's $300 of damage, you can probably handle that. But if you were to injure someone with your car, it could cost tens of thousands, or even hundreds of thousands of dollars. Auto insurance is designed to protect you from the possibility of financial ruin over a momentary lack of judgment.

If you got sick and missed two days of work it probably wouldn't be the end of the world. What if you became disabled and couldn't work for one or two years? Could you maintain your standard of living? Would you lose your home or car? Disability income insurance protects you from completely losing your standard of living in the event you are unable to work due to a serious illness or accident.

When a family is dependent on the income from one or both parents, and one of them dies, does that mean the rest of the family doesn't need money any longer? Is it likely they will still want a place to live, food to eat and clothes to wear? If the children were in a private school, it is probable this was important to their parents. Would they be able to stay in a private school? Where will the money come from? This is the purpose of life insurance. Insurance is for asset and risk management.

Life Insurance

There are two primary types of life insurance: term and cash value. There are many variations on these two types.

Term insurance is designed to provide the largest amount of death benefit at the lowest out of pocket cost in the early years. When a couple is young, raising a family, and has little disposable income, term insurance can be an appropriate choice. It provides the important protection at an affordable rate. As you get older and the term expires, the cost increases for the next renewal term. You can select coverage for terms of 1 year, 5 years, all the way to 30 years. The coverage can remain level, or the premium may remain level, but that has to be a trade-off.

When you stop paying premiums, the coverage ends and the money you spent is gone.

Life insurance has often been ridiculed as an investment vehicle. Its primary purpose was to provide ongoing support when an income earner died. It was not intended to be the investment vehicle of choice. There are many cases where it is the only structure that allows some people to save money. In recent years, it has become an investment alternative. It can be an incredible vehicle when used creatively in estate planning strategies. It can provide tax benefits in the form of a universal life or variable life investment product.

Cash Value insurance combines a savings element with the death benefit offered by term insurance. With this type, you pay more money for the same amount of coverage, but a portion of the premium is set aside in a separate fund which you can access, without having to die. It comes with names like whole life, universal life, variable life, endowments and more. Which is right for you? That depends on your situation. Are you single or married? Do you have children who are dependent on your income? Do you have parents who are dependent on your income? Do you have debts you would like paid off at death, instead of passing them on to family members? Are you in a business with someone where a death could cause a decline, or possible end to the continuation of the business? Do you expect to leave a large estate at death and would like to pay the death taxes at a discount? If you refer to the section on how to pick a financial planner, you can use those same questions to pick a life insurance agent. Start by asking people you respect for a referral.

What product would you use to solve the following situation? Make believe you're the head of a family with a spouse and two children, ages 6 and 8. You are in the fortunate situation where your career pays enough for your spouse to stay at home and care for the children. Your objectives are to begin a systematic investment program, protect your family if you die too soon, and set aside money for your children's college education. You're willing to take reasonable risks with your investments and want diversification like mutual funds offer. You don't like the tax hit from owning mutual funds personally (versus through a qualified retirement plan), and would like your investments to have some tax advantage.

Here's where a professional experienced insurance agent or financial planner becomes your ally or advisor. Should you get term insurance to protect your family or cash value insurance? Should you get a variable annuity to defer the taxes on the mutual funds or add to your 401(k) plan at work? What if you don't have a retirement plan at work? Should you get a universal life policy to have flexibility with the premiums? What about your investment goals?

One recommendation could be a Variable Universal Life insurance policy (VUL). This would provide the protection for your family, the mutual funds for your investment goals, and the tax advantages you're looking for. Again, I'm not going into detail here, that's the job of a financial planner or insurance agent.

Even though you have an idea of the product that could fit, how do you choose the company to purchase it from? There are over a hundred life insurance companies offering a VUL product. Again, this is the advantage of using a professional. You can spend your precious free time on the Internet getting quotes from dozens of companies; learn the ins and outs of each product; research the loads, actuarial assumptions and underlying portfolios; or you can have someone who has years of experience do it for you.

Health Insurance

Most people who have health insurance are covered through their employer or some government plan, like Medicare. Unfortunately almost one third of our population does not have health insurance. One serious health incident like cancer, stroke, heart attack or auto accident when there's no medical coverage, can drive a family into bankruptcy. This is one of the reasons the Affordable Health Care Act became law in 2013. I would urge you, if you don't already have major medical coverage, to do what it takes to get coverage. The higher the amount of the deductible (the portion you pay) the lower your premiums will be. Of course, the older you get, the more likely there will be health challenges, and the premiums will be higher.

Property Insurance

Property insurance differs from life and health insurance and is based on what you are protecting. In property, or casualty insurance, you are protecting things and not people; things like a car, house, boat, business and so on.

What are some of the things you should look for when shopping for property insurance? One would be for the company to be an "admitted carrier." I live in California, and in the 1990s there were many situations where people had purchased auto insurance from companies that had not been approved to do business in my state. They had the lowest rates, but when the policy owner had to file a claim, they didn't pay. Price is not the only factor when shopping for insurance. Look to the financial strength of the company. You're buying insurance to protect you against the things you can't afford to lose, right? The lowest premium, but denying claims doesn't work for building wealth. Ask, and get confirmation the company is admitted to do business in your state.

Will you be going direct to the company like 21st Century Insurance (now AIG) or GEICO? These are examples of direct writers. This is a company where you do business directly with the company and have no agent working on your behalf. You ought to save on the premiums with these types of companies. I have an insurance background, and going direct works for me. I don't need someone to explain policy features to me; I can read and understand the contract.

Will you be buying more than auto insurance with the company? As an example, one company I'm aware of, ANPAC, provides a refund feature if you insure both your home and auto insurance with them. They return 25% of your first year premium in the fourth year if you've gone without claims for three years, and do this year after year. In addition, if you also have your life insurance with them, they provide additional discounts. If you're going to purchase this coverage anyway, why not save as much as you can?

Finally, there are the value added services an agent can provide. The agent is someone who knows you and your situation. They have many other clients and can provide referrals to people in other specialties you might need, from cement masons to dentists. A unique service I ran across years ago was for parents who have children attending college. Some insurance agents sold a program that did a national search for various scholarships, grants, and other financial aid depending on the area of interest and the school the child had selected. Some programs even provided funds for adults (parents) who wanted to return to school and complete their education. These search programs typically cost $75 to $250, and often guaranteed finding educational funds of at least $500, or twice the money you paid. Speak with others before you put your money down; be sure they are legitimate and their guarantee will be honored.

Financial strength, being an admitted carrier, discounts, value-added benefits and the services of an agent or financial planner are some of the things to look for when you go shopping for life, health, or property insurance.

Real Estate

This is my favorite area of investing despite the recent housing and mortgage meltdown. That was actually the time to take advantage of the fire sales. Some people like to invest in single-family houses. I prefer apartment buildings. In the same way the stock market is highly subject to investor psychology, feelings, and emotions so are single-family houses. Apartment buildings are more insulated from emotions. When I purchase a building and make upgrades to increase rents, I directly increase the value of the building. If I bought it for 10 times the rental income, and double the rental income, I have doubled the value of the building, regardless of investor emotions.

Stocks and mutual funds are easier to invest in. You can start with small amounts of money. With real estate you need larger amounts of money, unless you use someone else's money. Many of the real estate seminars teach; how to find property and use other people's money to purchase it.

I am not Warren Buffett and when I buy stock I will have no influence on the board of directors, the products they develop or how they choose to market their products or services. I have control issues, and that is why real estate investing is comfortable for me. I get to choose the area I invest in, who the tenants are, what upgrades I will make and when I will sell the building. Buying and managing apartment buildings is what made me wealthy.

Peer to Peer Lending

The advent of the Internet has allowed people all over the world to connect through social media, and allowed the creation of peer to peer lending. One example is Lending Club where you can loan money to people in amounts as small as $25 and earn 6-12%. The minimum account size is $2500, and you must read the risks, but this could be an alternative to letting money sit in the bank.

Life Settlement Investing

This is a way to invest in life insurance policies that have been issued to other people. Cash value policies can be surrendered to the issuing company or sold on the open market for more money than the issuing company might pay. You would be taking over as the owner and beneficiary of the policy issued on the life of someone else. You would make the premium payments and at the death of the insured you would receive the death benefit. There are several companies that are set up to handle all of the paperwork and claim you can earn 14% or more with no stock market risk. To get an idea of how these companies operate you can google *life insurance settlement companies.*

Use the leverage of tax-advantaged investing

If you have the opportunity to invest in any type of qualified retirement plan, such as a *401(k), profit-sharing or pension plan, Tax Sheltered Annuities, or any tax qualified retirement plan,* take advantage of it. To see the difference of making investments on an after-tax basis or a tax-deferred basis, take a look at the next chart. Just be aware you want to discuss any potential tax liabilities you may have for your individual situation with your personal tax advisor. The middle columns are the accumulation totals.

Tax deductible contributions of $100 per month earning 10% for someone in a 30% tax bracket

	Paying your taxes along the way	Deferring your taxes	Difference
10 years	$12,116	$ 20,484	$ 8,368
20 years	$36,465	$ 75,937	$ 39,472
30 years	$85,398	$226,049	$140,651

As you can see, the impact over time of deferring taxes becomes significant. By year 30, the difference between $85,398 and $226,049 is 264%. Losing 30% in taxes at that time would reduce it to $158, 235. This is still $72,000 more than the amount available if taxes were paid along the way. That difference alone is enough to buy a brand new top-of-the-line Mercedes-Benz for all cash.

Don't pay your debts first!

By now I would expect you're in the mood and excited to begin setting aside money to create financial freedom. Besides, you deserve to pay yourself first. Many people who have credit card or short-term debt tell me at this point, "As soon as I pay off my debts I'll start to save and/or invest." This is faulty thinking, but it's not your fault. Do you remember when I explained the concept of "pay yourself first" with the two circles and said to start paying yourself first even if you have debt to pay off? In the section on "Becoming a Millionaire on $10 per Day," I provided a chart that showed the cost of waiting to invest. Now I'll provide similar information in the form of a story.

It seems the common wisdom from many accountants and financial advisors is to pay off your high interest debts before you start a savings or investment program. On the surface it might look appropriate, or even intelligent, to pay off credit card debt at 14% to 21% instead of putting money in a savings at 2% to 5%, or investing when the return could be unknown. To start with, if your credit is good, you can transfer balances to lower rate credit cards. If your objective is to create financial freedom where work as a choice and not a requirement, using the common wisdom may not be the best advice to take. See if you agree after I tell you the story of Jack and Jill.

After working with people and their money for about 40 years, I've discovered two sets of conflicting views. The first set is, *short term versus long term*; and the second is, *looks good on paper versus human nature*. The funny part, or sad part, depending on your personal outlook, is what looks good for the short term is a disaster for the long term. And, what looks good on paper most often does not fit how human beings act.

Let's introduce the characters of our story, Jack and Jill. (No relationship to the kids who were in the hill and water drama.) They are friends and work for the same company, and they both earn the same amount. Although Jill is the VP of sales and Jack is an administrative assistant, this is about the impact of compound earnings, not equal pay for equal work.

Both Jack and Jill spent money unconsciously for several years before they turned 35. Jack purchased stuff to impress other people and Jill bought clothing and jewelry she didn't need to fill the emptiness that welled up inside of her. (The sound you

167

hear is my guitar gently weeping.) They each built up $15,000 of credit card debt at 16% interest. What a coincidence!

> Jack's debt: $15,000 at 16% interest
> Payments of $300 per month:
> Total payoff: $24,883 in 83 months
> At $425 per month
> Total payoff: $20,405 in 48 months
> Saves 35 payments and $4,478.

Box 1

Jack was making payments of $300 per month, and he calculated his debt would be paid off in seven years. But, by adding an additional $125 per month he could eliminate three years of payments and save himself about $4,500 in interest (see Box 1). He said after he paid off his credit cards in four years, then he would invest the $125 per month. After all, he was paying 16% interest and if he put his money in a bank at 5–6%, or even if he could get 12% in a mutual fund, he was guaranteed a 16% return just by paying off his debt. His CPA said it was the best thing to do, but they were only looking at the short term, not the long term.

Jill, the smart one, had listened to my *"Wealth on Any Income"* CD program and decided to pay herself first by putting money in a high quality mutual fund which had average earnings of 12% annually for several decades. (She could have purchased a variable annuity, made direct stock purchases and paid no commissions, or even contributed to her company's 401(k) plan, but I want to keep my example simple.)

Projecting out into the future, if Jill made monthly contributions of $125 (or about $4.17 per day) for 28 years at 12% earnings, by age 63 she would have accumulated $341,400. Jack, on the other hand delayed his investing for four years until he paid off his credit cards. By age 63 he would have $207,000, or $134,400 less than Jill. His waiting four years and saving

$4,500 in credit card interest cost him $134,400 in lost earnings over the next 24 years (see Box 2).

While Jill's results look good on paper, the difficulty is with human nature. Most people lack the discipline to set aside money on a regular basis. I'm suggesting a difference of only $4.17 per day will create these wonderful results over 24 to 28 years. However, most bank Christmas clubs opened in January are emptied by the end of the summer. A structure that almost forces people to pay themselves first might be the most important foundation to creating financial freedom. Vehicles like 401(k) plans, tax-sheltered annuities, variable life insurance, or dollar-cost-averaging into a mutual fund by payroll deduction could be considered as a better approach to reaching your goals than willpower.

> Jack's accumulation of $125 per month for
> 24 years at 12% earnings: $207,016
> Jill's accumulation of $125 per month for 28
> years at 12% earnings: $341.409
> Difference: $134,394

Box 2

At 2014 costs, the **difference** in cash is enough for Jill to go to Germany, pay for all the travel expenses, purchase a new Mercedes-Benz 500 SL convertible, bring it home and have enough to buy a Lexus, too. Instead of buying these goodies with the difference, if Jill used the earnings alone (over $16,000 per year), she could take a friend on vacation with her to Hawaii for a full week, including airfare, three times per year for the rest of her life, and have $2,000 spending cash on each trip.

Jack's accumulation of $125 per month for
24 years at 9% earnings: $126,692
Jill's accumulation of $125 per month for 28
years at 9% earnings: $188,538
Difference: $61,846

Box 3

If Jill earned only 9%, instead of 12%, she'd have accumulated $61,800 more than Jack. If Jill used the earnings from the *difference* (at 9%) it would allow her to go to Europe for two weeks, twice per year, pay for airfare, hotels, tours, and have $600 spending cash on each trip (see Box 3).

Please be aware of another assumption upon which I based this story: ONLY the $125 difference was considered for the calculations. There is no way to know if Jack will add the $300 per month extra to his investments after he pays off his credit cards, three year before Jill pays off her credit cards. (Even if he did do this, he would only produce $5,224 more than Jill, but he would have invested $10,800 more to do it.) Human nature has shown me 95% of the population won't add the extra $300 on a consistent monthly basis even when they say they will.

The moral of this story about Jack and Jill can be expressed by the German phrase *habeas achtoom corpus*: "Wash your hands before eating," or: don't wait to pay off your debts before you begin to invest. Pay yourself first *now*, or the delay will cost you far more than you'll save.

How to Guard Against Investment Fraud

Intelligence, education, success in business or a profession does not offer protection against being defrauded. Chances are the more successful you become, the more you will be able to attract a better class of con artist. I started collecting articles in 1983 and have dozens covering all sorts of frauds and swindles. They depict well- dressed, church-going, public and community involved individuals (Bernie Madoff), as well as gangsters, who stole from the people who trusted them. Some of the following information was taken from a Sylvia Porter article dated 9-14-88, and things have not changed much in the last sixteen years. You can avoid being a victim of investment fraud by following these guidelines:

- Develop a coherent investment strategy tailored to your own circumstances. The development of realistic investment goals is worth the effort, not only for its own sake, but also because it results in a healthy skepticism that con artists dread.

- Select investments to fit *your* goals. Do not settle for what someone wants to sell you. Even in times of economic uncertainty, solid investment opportunities exist.

- Choose a professional advisor as carefully as you would select a million dollar investment. Refer to the questions on how to pick an advisor in a previous section.

- Keep your guard up. Be aware that there are people who want to live well on your money and they may look and sound as respectable as anybody else.

- Have a good defensive strategy. Use other professionals you trust to review investment offerings in which they have expertise. Ask an insurance agent about insurance; ask a CPA tax questions; ask a stockbroker about a specific stock; ask an attorney a legal question; ask a certified financial planner to help you set goals. You wouldn't ask your gardener for medical advice. Would you?

- NEVER, EVER, AND I MEAN *NEVER* SEND MONEY, OR GIVE YOUR CREDIT CARD NUMBER, TO A STRANGER ON THE BASIS OF A PHONE CALL, ESPECIALLY IF THEY SAY THEY ARE WITH THE IRS.

- Before investing in a new stock offering, read the prospectus—especially if the promoter tells you not to bother.

- Don't take exaggerated promises at face value. If such great returns are real, why would they share the secret?
- Do not be hustled by high-pressure tactics. The investment world is not going to run out of good opportunities in the next hour.
- Beware of hucksters who claim they're doing you a favor because you're a member of a particular organization, church, or a group.
- Do not assume state or federal regulators can protect you. They are far outnumbered by the scam artists.

Other Frauds: Charities

There are other frauds of which to be aware. In an Ann Landers column reported in the Los Angeles Times on April 19, 1998, charities can be deceptive and misleading, too. A company that used to go by the name of Watson & Hughey, which was changed to Direct Response Consulting Services, used sweepstakes and telemarketing to raise money, supposedly for charities. In some cases, nearly all of the money raised was kept by Watson & Hughey. Over the last several decades, the Attorney General of many states brought suit against phony charities, probably resulting in their changing their names, but not their practices. The charities have legitimate-sounding names as part of the deception. Here is a partial list of the charities to stay away from:

- American Institute for Cancer Research (sounds like American Cancer Society)
- National Children's Cancer Society
- Center for Advanced Heart Research
- Center for Alternative Cancer Research
- United Children's Fund
- A Child's Wish (sounds like Make A Wish Foundation)
- National Cancer Research Institute
- United Way *

* It appears that the United Way in Connecticut may be complicit in a hoax involving the Sandy Hook Elementary School shootings. Please Google *Sandy Hook United Way* and determine this for yourself.

To protect yourself, do not give money to a charity with which you are not completely familiar, to a paid solicitation firm, or to a paid solicitor. Read the fine print on their material or ask the caller if they are working for a paid solicitor. At http://www.charitynavigator.org you can check how well they spend their donations.

Conclusion

As I discussed in the beginning of this book, with Awareness, Tools and Actions you can create financial prosperity, even in a roller coaster economy. You are now aware of how millionaires operate; you've become aware of your beliefs, where they've come from and your values. You used the tools like the Balance Sheet and Cash Flow Form to provide awareness of your money. The Spending Plan Register provides awareness on a moment's notice of where your money is going and if you're getting the level of pleasure you're paying for. Using these tools is taking action. Speaking with other people and letting them support you is action at the highest level to produce results. Creating accountability with another person is setting up the action structure to produce results. If you haven't started working on the forms in the back of the book, now is the time. As you continue on your path to financial abundance, prosperity and freedom, please share what you've learned with others. You'll all be glad you did. Congratulations on completing this book.

I wish you the best in life, and to live the life you love.

—Rennie Gabriel

Your attitude and actions of the past have brought you to where you are today.

Your attitude and actions today will create your future.

– Rennie Gabriel

Appendix

In this section, you'll find the tools that have been described throughout the book. Instead of writing in this book, I recommend you make photocopies of the forms for your personal use. In that way, you can use them again from time to time to see your progress.

YOUR PERSONAL INFORMATION

Date _____

Name (Person #1) _____
Address _____
City _____ State _____ Zip _____
Place of Birth _____

Wk Phone ( ) _____
Hm Phone ( ) _____

Soc Sec _____
Birth Date _____

(Person #2)
Significant Other _____
Place of Birth _____
Soc Sec _____
Children _____ age _____
_____ _____
_____ _____

Wk Phone ( ) _____
Birth Date _____
Wedding date _____
If married, their mate's name & age:
_____ _____
_____ _____

Person #1 Employer _____
Position _____
Address _____

Person #2 _____
Position _____
Address _____

Income $ _____

Income $ _____

COMPANY BENEFITS PROVIDED

Group Life _____
Disability _____
Health _____
Retirement _____
Other _____

176

Accountant _____

Firm _____

Address _____

Phone (___) _____

Provides tax advice, or just prepares tax return?

Insurance Agent _____

Co./ Firm _____

Address _____

City, State, Zip _____

Phone (___) _____

Attorney _____

Firm _____

Address _____

Phone (___) _____

Stock Broker _____

Firm _____

Address _____

City, State, Zip _____

Phone (___) _____

PERTINENT INFORMATION

Current Will? Y/N Date _____ Trusts? Y/N _____ Living Trust? Y/N Date _____ Prenuptial? Y/N _____

#1 Health: Smoker? Y/N _____ Medical situations _____ Drugs Used: _____

#2 Health: Smoker? Y/N _____ Medical situations _____ Drugs Used: _____

Safe Deposit Box _____ Location _____

Alimony obligations? Y/N _____ Describe: _____

#1 Parents living? (Ages) Mom _____ Dad _____   #2 Parents living? (Ages) Mom _____ Dad _____

Parent's Health _____

Their Financial Status _____

Inheritance Someday $ _____ $ _____

Person #1: Number of: brothers _____ sisters _____   #2: Number of: brothers _____ sisters _____

177

TOOL #1 - THE DEBT ELIMINATION FORM

Complete this form by placing the lowest balance owed at the top of the list and work down to the highest balance. Send any extra money to pay off creditors, beyond your minimum payment, to only the one at the top of the list until they are paid off. Then move down to the next one on the list.

CREDITOR	BALANCE OWED	APR%	MIN. PAYMENT	PAYMENT MADE

Total Credit Card Debt $ _____
Transfer this figure to Tool #2 where shown.

Total Min. Pmts. $ _____
Transfer this figure to Tool #3 and/or 3a, line 16.

"Credit supports agriculture the way a rope supports a hanged man." While this quote from Louis XIV was about farming, you could guess it would apply to any business or individual.

TOOL #2 - BALANCE SHEET

ASSETS

Home (FMV)* $ _____

Other Real Estate _____

Other Real Estate _____

Personal Property _____

Vested Retirement _____

IRAs _____

Listed Securities _____

Stock Options _____

Life Ins. (Cash Value) _____

Business Interest -

Accts. Receivable _____

Inventory/Equip. _____

Cash/Retained Earn. _____

Goodwill _____

Personal Savings _____

Money Mkt Acct _____

LIABILITIES

Home Mortgage (s) $ _____

Other R.E. Loans _____

_____

_____

From Tool #1: Credit Cards $ _____
(Other items: Auto loan, boat, notes, family loans, pool loan, past income taxes, etc.)

Other Items: $ _____

_____

_____

_____

TOTAL LIAB. $ _____

180

CD's -

Next Maturity Date _____

Checking account _____

Autos _____

Other _____

TOTAL ASSETS $ _____

NET WORTH $ _____

* FMV: Fair Market Value

HOME DETAILS

Purchase Price _____   Date _____   Remaining Payments _____

Interest Rate _____ %   Fixed _____   Variable _____

181

TOOL #3 - THE CASH FLOW FORM (Complete based on monthly calculations)

INCOME	EXPENSE Person # _____

INCOME		EXPENSE
Person #1: _____ (1)		1. House Pmt. /Rent _____
Person #2: _____		(Other house exp., maid, gardener) _____
Bonus _____		18. Property Taxes _____ *
Commission _____		13. Other RE Loans _____
Rents _____		18. Other RE Taxes _____ *
Interest _____		Other RE Expense _____
Dividends _____		2. Auto: Loans/Lease _____
Notes Rcvd. _____		Parking/Gas _____
Royalties _____		Maint./Repairs _____ *
Side Business _____		Regist. Fees _____ *
Trust Distribution _____		3.Food:
		Groceries _____
Social Security _____		Meals Out _____
Retirement Plan _____		4. Clothing _____ *
Other _____		5. Personal Care _____
		6. Health Care _____
		7. Entertainment _____
The above figures are:		8. Gifts _____ *
Monthly _____		9. Education _____
Annual _____		10. Vacations _____ *
		11. Business Expense _____ **

182

Pay Periods are:
1 time mo. _____
2 times mo. _____
Every 2 wks. _____
Disability _____ *
(1) Is this a net or gross income figure? _____
Gross: Prior to taxes and deductions.
Net: After taxes and deductions.
If this is a net figure, you don't
Have to complete #18 Taxes
under the Expenses. Also, don't
include other deductions like
health insurance, if that's taken out.

TOTAL $ _____

12. Dependent Care _____
13. Invest/Systematic Save _____
    Qualified Retirement Plan _____
14. Insurance: Life _____ *
    Auto _____ *
    Health _____
    Home/Apt. _____ *
15. Charitable _____
16. Debt Pmt/ Charge Accts _____
17. Utilities: Gas _____
    Water/Power _____
    Telephone _____
    Trash/Other _____
18. Income Taxes: Federal _____
    State _____

TOTAL $ _____

SURPLUS / DEFICIT $ _____

*These may be expenses that do not show up each month, but need to be set aside monthly.
** From the Business Income & Expense Statement

TOOL #3A - Use this form for a couple to split expenses.

Person #1 Monthly Net Income $ _____
Person #2 Monthly Net Income $ _____
Total Income avail. for expenses $ _____

For (Month/Year): _____

Choose who will be responsible for how much of each item.

	Projected	Person #1	Person #2
1. House Pmt/Rent	_____	_____	_____
(Other house exp., maid, gardener)	_____ *	_____	_____
18. Property Taxes	_____	_____	_____
13. Other Real Estate Loans	_____	_____	_____
Other RE Taxes	_____ *	_____	_____
Other RE Expense	_____	_____	_____
2. Auto: Loans/Lease	_____	_____	_____
Parking/Gas	_____	_____	_____
Maintenance/Repairs	_____ *	_____	_____
Registration Fees	_____ *	_____	_____
3. Food: Groceries	_____	_____	_____
Meals Out	_____	_____	_____
4. Clothing	_____ *	_____	_____
5. Personal Care	_____	_____	_____
6. Health Care	_____	_____	_____
7. Entertainment	_____	_____	_____
8. Gifts	_____ *	_____	_____

184

9. Education

10. Vacations   *

11. Business Expense

12. Dependent Care

13. Invest/Systematic Save

    Qualified Retirement Plan

14. Insurance: Life   *

    Auto   *

    Disability   *

    Health

    Home/Apartment   *

15. Charitable

16. Debt Pmt/Charge Accts   (Tool #1)

17. Utilities: Gas

    Water/Power

    Telephone

    Trash/Other

20. Legal/Accounting

        TOTALS: $_____ $_____ $_____

*These are the expenses which might not show up monthly, but need to be set aside monthly.

The totals at the bottom of Person #1 and #2 should equal the total from the first column.
The totals also need to be less than the income shown above. (Duh!) If it's not, refer back to Step 9 in the book, "What to do when expenses exceed income."

185

Tool #4 - CASH FLOW MEMORY JOGGER

You can tear out the following pages or copy it to carry with you. It will remind you of the categories the different expenses fall into. When you sit down and fill in the Cash Flow Form and can't remember all the places you could be spending your money, it will remind you. As an example someone might say, "I don't buy clothes. I don't have any expense there." But they do if they go to the dry cleaners or laundry. Those are clothing expenses. There should be no "miscellaneous" items. If it's not on the list, and it's legal, call me and let me know what it is.

1. Home/Shelter
A. Mortgage or Rent
B. Miscellaneous
C. Maintenance
D. Gardener/Maid
E. Purchases
F. Home Assoc. Dues
G. Alarm Service
2. Auto/Transpor-tation
A. Car payment/ lease
B. Gasoline/fuel
C. Parking
D. Registration
E. Oil/Lube
F. Maintenance
G. Repair
H. Accessories
I. Bus/Taxi
J. Airfare
K. Other
3. Food
A. Groceries
B. Meals Out
C. Snacks
4. Clothing
A. Apparel
B. Shoes
C. Accessories
D. Jewelry
E. Tailor
F. Cleaners
G. Laundry
H. Shoe repair
I. Jewelry repair
5. Personal Care
A. Toiletries
B. Cosmetics
C. Manicures

D. Pedicures
E. Hair cuts/colors
F. Massage
G. Spa/Gym
6. Health Care
A. Doctor
B. Dentist
C. Chiropractor
D. Eyewear
E. Ophthalmologist
F. Optometrist
G. Podiatrist
H. Prescriptions
I. Vitamins
J. Psychologist
7. Entertainment/
   Recreation
A. Recreation
B. Books
C. Cable TV
D. Clubs/Dancing
E. Athletics, Concerts,
   Sporting Events
F. Hobbies
G. Houseguests
H. Liquor/
   Smoking
I. Magazines
J. Movies
K. Music/CD's
L. Sightseeing,
M. Theater
N. Video
   Purchase/Rental
8. Gifts
A. Anniversaries
B. Birthdays
C. Cards

D. Chanukah
E. Christmas
F. Easter
G. Flowers
H. Love Gifts
I. Weddings
9. Education
A. Books
B. Classes
C. Fees/Supplies
D. Seminars/Workshops
E. Tapes
F. Tuition
10. Vacations
A. Special Interest
B. Summer
C. Winter
D. Weekends
E. Travel Fund
11. Business Expenses
   (see Business form)
12. Dependent Care
A. Alimony
B. Auto
C. Child Care/ Support
D. Clothing
E. Daycare
F. Family Events
G. Food
H. Insurance
I. Medical
J. Pet Care
K. Schools
L. Services
M. Supplies
13. Regular Save/Invest
A. Bonds
B. Mutual Funds

C. Real Estate
D. Stocks
E. Savings Account
F. Retirement Plan
G. TSA / IRA
14. Insurance
A. Auto
B. Disability Income
C. Health
D. Home/Apartment
E. Life Insurance
15. Spiritual Charity
A. Contributions
B. Hand-outs
C. 7th Tradition
D. Seminars

E. Tithing
16. Debt Repayment
Charge Account
    Payments
A. Bank Credit Cards
B. Dept. Store Charges
C. Family Loans
D. Student Loans
E. Trust Deeds
F. Other
17. Utilities
A. Water
B. Power/Electric
C. Gas/Propane
D. Garbage
E. Phone/Cell/Pager

F. Internet
18. Taxes
A. Federal Income
B. State Income
C. Social Security
D. Property/Home
E. Other Real Estate
F. Business (see #11)
G. City/County
H. Other
19. Lessons Learned
A. Money Lost or
    Wasted
20. Legal or
Accounting Fees

FREE SPENDING PLAN REGISTER

Instead of copying and assembling your own Spending Plan Register from the book, get one for FREE.

☐ Yes, please send me one FREE Spending Plan Register.

☐ I'd like to order a set of 12 Spending Registers for $14.00 + $4:00- S&H

Name _____

Address _____

City, State, Zip _____

Daytime phone (   )   -

☐ FREE REGISTER

Fax order to (818) 936-6837 or mail to:
The Financial Coach, Inc.
5101 Sophia Ave.
Encino, CA 91436

☐ Set of 12 for $18.00, enclose check, or charge on VISA or MC

CC # _____ exp date _____

Signature: _____

TOOL #5—THE FINANCIAL COACH™ SPENDING PLAN REGISTER

You can make copies of this form and insert it in with your checkbook register or in your wallet or purse. Two copies are provided for you here.

Category				Category			
____ plan to spend			$____	____ plan to spend			$____
cash			____	cash			____
credit			____	credit			____
check	Date	Notes	amount	check	Date	Notes	amount

Category				Category			
____		plan to spend	$____	____		plan to spend	$____
cash			____	cash			____
credit			____	credit			____
check	Date	Notes	amount	check	Date	Notes	amount